CRYSTALS

For All Seasons and Reasons

by
Ileana Abrev

CRYSTALS
For All Seasons and Reasons
Copyright © 2025 by Ileana Abrev
All rights reserved.
ISBN: 978-1-7640294-6-9 Paperback
ISBN: 978-1-7640294-7-6 E-Book

No portion of this book may be reproduced in any form without written permission from the publisher or author.

DISCLAIMER:
The Content of this book is not a substitute for medical attention, treatment, examination, advice or diagnosis. This book is not intended to provide a clinical diagnosis nor take the place of proper medical advice from a fully qualified medical practitioner.

The author does not take any responsibility for any possible consequences from actions taken by the reader from this book and should always take medical advice from a general practitioner

Published with the assistance of
ANGEL KEY PUBLICATIONS
https://angelkey.com.au/index.html

A catalogue record for this book is available from the National Library of Australia

CONTENTS

Crystals, The Myth	1		Ametrine	64
Minerals 101	5		Apache Tear	65
How Do Crystals Work	11		Apatite	66
Choosing A Crystal	17		Apophyllite	67
Cleansing Your Crystal	23		Aquamarine	68
Programming Crystals	27		Aventurine	70
The Healing Shapes of Crystals	31		Azurite	72
			Azurite With Malachite	73
Scrying	37		Bloodstone	74
Crystal Readings	**41**		Blue Quartz	75
Initiating A New Way of Life	51		Calcite	76
			Carnelian Agate	77
Crystals A-Z	**55**		Cat's Eye	78
			Celestine	79
Agate	56		Charoite	80
Alexandrite	58		Chalcopyrite	81
Amazonite	59		Chrysocolla	82
Amber (Resin)	60		Chrysoprase	83
Amethyst	62			

Citrine	84	Moldavite	108
Clear Quartz	85	Moonstone	109
Copal (Resin)	87	Obsidian and Snowflake Obsidian	111
Coral (Shell)	88		
Diamond	89	Onyx	113
Emerald	90	Opal	114
Fluorite	91	Pearl (Oyster Shell)	115
Garnet	92	Peridot	116
Hematite	93	Petrified Wood (Fossil)	118
Howlite	94	Pyrite (Fool's Gold)	119
Iolite	95	Rhodochrosite	120
Jade	96	Rhodonite	121
Jasper (Red)	98	Rose Quartz	122
Jet (Wood Fossilised)	100	Ruby	123
Kunzite	101	Rutilated Quartz	125
Labradorite	102	Sapphire	126
Lapis Lazuli	103	Selenite	127
Lazurite	104	Serpentine	128
Lepidolite	105	Smoky Quartz	129
Loadstone	106	Sodalite	130
Malachite	107	Sugilite	131

Sunstone	132	Silver	149
Tiger Eye	133	Crystal Zodiac Signs	151
Tiger Iron	135	Crystals and	
Topaz	136	The Chakras	161
Tourmalinated Quartz	138	Crystals For The Home	175
Turquoise	139	A Crystal For Each Day	
Unakite	141	Of The Week	179
Zeolite	142	Closing	185
Zircon	143	A Quick Reference Guide	
Metals	**145**	to Crystal Healing	187
Copper	146	Bibliography	223
Gold	147		
Meteorite	148		

The love of precious crystals is deeply imparted in the human heart, and the cause of this must be sought not only in their colouring and brilliance, but also their durability.

All the fair colours of flowers and foliage and even the blue of the sky and the glory of the sunset clouds only last for a short time and are subject to continual change. But the sheen and colouration of precious crystals are the same today as they were thousands of years ago and will be for thousands of years to come. In a world of change, this permanence has a charm of its own that was early appreciated.

—George Frederick Kunz, 1913

*To my grandchildren
Emmett and Clara.*

Crystals, The Myth

Before minerals were mined, they were cultured for adornment, magic, medicinal purposes, and to attract wealth and power. Every ancient civilisation has used crystals. Lore suggests that crystals were a big part of the Atlanteans, who focused on healing and higher spiritual enlightenment. They were also an essential tool for Egyptians to make vases, utensils, and figurines for their deities, not to mention crushing Lapis Lazuli for eye makeup.

In medieval times, a Bloodstone Crystal was wrapped around a wound dressing to stop bleeding. Holistically, today, a Bloodstone Crystal is used for people who have haemophilia or any bleeding disorder. In ancient Greece, it was said you would not get drunk if you drank wine out of an Amethyst mug. It was believed that Hematite was the crystal of invisibility. Today, Hematite aids you in reaching your goals and promotes courage and strength to achieve them.

American Indians used Azurite to call their spirits, and China believed in the power of Jade for love, healing, and the making of musical instruments. When a Jade crystal was worn, it gave the wearer unlimited wealth. Today, Jade is used spiritually for wealth and is still a big part of their culture.

Ancient faith and beliefs in Crystal healing and magical powers for protection, strength, or medicinal purposes were never frowned upon. In ancient times, no one disputed when a Rose Quartz crystal was given to a child with respiratory problems. No questions were asked when Amber, a resin, was crushed and mixed with honey to alleviate sore throats and pain. Amber is now used mostly as a necklace for children who are teething. Mothers swear by this method, which alleviates the teething process.

The legacy of crystals is stronger than ever before. Crystals are infinite and used for everything that ails, worries, and makes us sick. Crystals are also an excellent complementary tool when used with conventional medicine.

Crystals' meanings are channelled by psychic work and some through a crystal's composition. For example, Spodumene is a Pyroxene mineral filled with a Lithium compound found in a Kunzite crystal. In the medical field, Lithium is used for mental health. Because Kunzite has Lithium, its meaning is to aid people with their mental health conditions, such as anxiety, and anything related to those illnesses.

The colour of a crystal also helps you identify its healing qualities, like pink crystals for love or self-love, purple for stress, yellow for learning, and so on. Lastly, there are also generations' worth of meanings that still stand to this date.

So many ancient civilisations have used crystals, and I ask you, 'How could so many be wrong?' This tells us, 'If it worked then, why can't it work now?'

Each generation brings something sacred to the next. This is true with crystals.

Let us listen, heal, and learn from them as our ancestors did.

Minerals 101

Minerals, metals, and rocks become Crystals when they crystallise within a mineral. There are a few ways this can take place. One of the most common ways is when water evaporates from the internal spaces. These crystals are volcanic in origin. When hot molten rock, which is magma, cools off, the rock will crystallise. Small crystals form if it cools quickly, and if it cools slowly, bigger crystals form.

Crystals can also form when the Earth folds. This kind of pressure can change their structure.

There are precious and semiprecious 'rocks'. The precious are Diamonds, Rubies, and Sapphires, which are at the top of the list of hardness according to the Mohs scale, being one — the softest and — ten the hardest. Then there are the semiprecious stones we all know as Amethyst, Clear Quartz, or Agates. These are in the middle of the solidity list, which goes all the way down to Talc, which is the softest mineral on the Mohs scale coming in at one.

The history of our evolution has been categorised into minerals, metals, and rock stages.

- **Stone Age**: We used rocks for tools. Spears were crafted out of Obsidian. We lived in caves to protect us from the elements and animals of proportional sizes.

- **Copper Age**: We learned how to melt minerals with heat.
- **Bronze Age**: We learned how to mix minerals by melting and smelting them.
- **Iron Age:** We learned how to make tools and implements out of metal to build structures, buildings, roads, consumables, and even artefacts.

Today, minerals and rocks are essential in our daily lives. If it doesn't come from a plant or an animal, it comes from a mineral mined and extracted adequately for usage.

Unfortunately, we take for granted where our everyday resources are extracted from or for.

Quartz is a good example. There is a large variety of Quartz, like Citrine, Amethyst, and Smoky Quartz. Then there are Agates, Jaspers, and even Onyx. These all belong to the Chalcedony family; some can produce electricity when subjected to mechanical stress. This process is called the piezoelectric effect, and quartz has the compound within it to do it. Quartz is used in radio transmitters, electronic clocks, resonators, and wave stabilisers. It is used in manufacturing glass, even paints and abrasives, not bad for such a simple crystal!

Like Quartz, there are many others. Pyrite is manufactured for sulphur and used to recover Iron, Gold, and Copper. Silver is used in many industrial applications, including jewellery, as we all know, and electronic and circuit boards. Diamonds, the industrial type, are used in machinery and mineral services for abrasives, construction, drilling, and transportation equipment.

Then there is Iron Ore, best known to all of us as Hematite, which is used for practically everything: cosmetics, plastics, radioactive medicine, and even polishing compounds. Fluorite is categorised as four on the Mohs scale. It has many uses, such as in the production of hydrofluoric acid, which is used in pottery, optical, ceramics, electroplating, and metal smelting.

Arsenical minerals, like arsenolite, orpiment, and arsenopyrite, have long been used in medicine. Even though they can be very toxic and carcinogenic, they are used in Promyelocytic Leukaemia patients. Arsenical minerals were also used in the treatment of syphilis, which antibiotics have superseded. In the modern age, arsenic compounds are used to produce pesticides and herbicides.

There are numerous ways minerals are used in our everyday life, too many to mention. I'm not a mineralogist, but the next time you sit at home, look around you, and if it is not made from a tree or an animal, whatever is left is made from minerals.

Those objects in your home were living radiant energies that have now been processed, smelted, mixed, and drilled to create our commodity, which we unconsciously take for granted. I'm not saying go and hug your refrigerator. Your fridge is mineral-based, forged hundreds of years ago, so maybe clean your fridge a bit more and respect your belongings as they have been centuries in the making; maybe see them as fossils because they are.

How Do Crystals Work

To have a crystal is to have a deeper understanding of yourself and the world around you. A crystal warms and hugs the soul. A new faith within you is born, and a new respect for the soul is found, but they are still a mystery, even to those who've made that connection.

Their consciousnesses are yet to be unravelled, but we know that if a Clear Quartz crystal can conduct energy and make a radio work, we can certainly use that same energy to enhance our Etheric field, which can be proven with dowsing rods.

Dowsing rods have been used for centuries. Historically, people have employed dowsing rods to locate metals; some people still use them to search for water. Unfortunately, there is no scientific evidence to support their effectiveness. However, I can assure you that individuals would not continue using them if they did not yield some results.

Years ago, I conducted an experiment using borrowed L-shaped dowsing rods. I had a friend stand very still while I began the experiment. Holding one rod in each hand, I tried to keep them as straight as possible, concentrating as I slowly walked toward her. Initially, nothing happened, but as I got closer, the dowsing rods began to turn inward. When I was about two feet from her, the rods crossed completely, forming an X. This indicated that her etheric field extended to only about two feet.

I gave her a Clear Quartz crystal to hold and began the same process again. This time, the rods closed inwards, creating another X approximately five feet away from her. The energy of the Clear Quartz amplified her Etheric field, strengthening her aura. This enhancement provided better protection against negativity from others and offered a stronger defence against sickness.

Imagine if you carried or wore a crystal all the time. Their energies would work in unison within each individual according to their needs and vibrational frequency. As the energy of crystals merges with our own, sparks fly into the Universe, and a wish is made in the heavens through spirit with one of the oldest living energies on Earth.

Crystals transmit a feeling of peace. A sense of spiritual enlightenment warms the heart. Anger becomes a thing of the past; you exude love and compassion toward those around you, and you learn to accept life's ups and downs.

Brain activity can be enhanced with the use of crystals. When you believe in something wholeheartedly, to the point where doubts do not creep into your mind, or if you have a desire that burns so passionately, anything is possible. Carrying a crystal reinforces the power of your belief, as it serves as a reminder of your intent to achieve your goal.

Do crystals really work? The answer is 'yes'. Give them a try and see for yourself. There is no harm in experimenting, regardless of your faith or beliefs. By using crystals, you connect with energies that extend beyond our current understanding; you have nothing to lose.

I've seen people give up when they don't see any improvement in meeting their needs. However, you'll never discover what's possible if you give up. We are all different, and we resonate with different frequencies. It's simply a matter of trying and trying until you connect with the special crystal that works for you.

Children are naturally more receptive to the mystical qualities of crystals. They often smell them and hold them close to their ears to see if they produce any sounds. I love seeing their eyes light up when I say, "Give these little crystals to the fairies; they always need them to build or decorate their homes." Parents tell me that when they return home, the children place the crystals in the garden and call out to the fairies. To their delight, most of the crystals had disappeared by the following morning.

If you cannot conceive that crystals can make a difference in your life, it may be because you are not in tune with your energy or the energies surrounding you. When you are ready to open yourself to the mystical power of crystals, go to a place with a wide range to choose from and allow your intuition to guide you to the crystal you need. Always keep an open mind and remember that not only are you searching for a specific crystal to help you attain your goal, but that crystal is also searching for you.

Choosing A Crystal

You can find crystals anywhere, from a new age store, a lapidary club, or a natural science museum with a gift shop. Once you've identified where to go, head there to find the right crystal for your current needs. Once you arrive, stand in front of the available crystals. Take a moment to close your eyes and meditate for a few minutes. This will help you connect with your inner self and focus on your deepest needs and desires.

When ready, open your eyes and look at the crystals again. The crystals could be of different shapes, sizes, colours, or mineral content for you to choose from. Still, there will be one… one that particularly attracts you and appears to call out, "Take me home!" If this crystal is small and worth only a few dollars, it doesn't mean it is less potent than a larger one. Size doesn't matter, but the affinity you feel for a crystal is paramount.

Some people feel a crystal warm or cold. Touching it may even send a tingling sensation up your arm. Some crystals have been known to cause numbness in the hands, a sudden surge of energy, light-headedness, or internal peace and tranquillity. When you pick and hold the crystal that attracts you, you make a spiritual connection between you, Mother Nature, and the Universe.

No experience is the same. Everybody has a different story when connecting with a particular crystal. No matter what you've read or know, you feel different for the first time in years. Sometimes people say, 'Wow, I never knew they felt like this,' or 'Yes, I can feel tingling up my arm,' but no matter what they say, a smile always follows.

The colour of a crystal is an essential aspect of its power, as it enhances your energy field to help strengthen and manifest your needs. Sometimes, crystals may lose their vibrancy. This fading can occur when the crystal is used to draw a lot of energy, particularly if it has been programmed to relieve stress. When this happens, the crystal is operating at its full potential. Fortunately, the crystal's original colour can be restored by cleansing it in sunlight.

Distributors of semi-precious crystals worldwide often enhance the colour of crystals using dye solutions and heat. However, this colour tends to fade after a few months of wear. In one instance, a woman commented that a crystal had darkened shortly after she held it. I advised her to set the crystal down, and she did, picking up a Rose Quartz instead. She held it, and the colour remained unchanged when she opened her hand. I stood beside her as she chose another crystal, a green Tourmaline. I paid special attention to its colour, which was light to medium green.

When she opened her hand, the crystal was much darker—a deeper green would have been my guess. She looked at me and asked how that was possible. I told her there could be numerous reasons why: the acidity in her hand, heat, as crystals do change colour when heated with special solutions, or simply a miraculous affiliation with the actual crystal. She told me it was all too spooky for her and left.

Sometimes, we struggle to find that special crystal, often because we are trying too hard. With so many options available, the meanings can be overwhelming. However, don't give up! I have a method that uses numerology to help you choose the crystal you need, along with a simple chart. This approach can also assist you in selecting a crystal for a friend if you're unsure what they might benefit from.

I have picked nine of the most popular crystals. You can find which crystal is best for you by following the easy numerology chart below.

Crystal	Number	Letters
Garnet	1	A – J – S
Carnelian	2	B – K – T
Tiger Eye	3	C – L – U
Aventurine	4	D – M – V
Sodalite	5	E – N – W
Amethyst	6	F – O – X
Rose Quartz	7	G – P – Y
Clear Quartz	8	H – Q - Z
Agate (All Colours)	9	I – R

e.g. my Name, Ileana Abrev. Break down the name as below. Then, under the name, the number that pertains to the letter as seen on the chart.

I L E A N   A A B R E V
9 3 5 1 5   1 1 2 9 5 4

Now add all the numbers in the above row
= 45

Then break this number again. 4 and 5 = 9

So, nine is an Agate.

This method can be used if you think you are not using the correct crystals; it will lead you to the right one for your needs.

Cleansing Your Crystal

Crystals can absorb and emit energy. Think of crystals as vacuum cleaners. A vacuum cleaner picks up unwanted dust and dirt from floors and carpets. Crystals, on the other hand, pick up a wide range of positive and negative energies.

When you touch a crystal, your energy is transferred into it and remains there until the crystal is cleansed again. Therefore, cleansing your new crystal should be your first step before using it. This process eliminates any negative energy that may have been absorbed from anyone who has come into contact with the crystal before you, including the retail staff who sold it to you, the people who previously sold it to them, the suppliers, and so on, all the way back to when it was first discovered.

There are many ways to cleanse a crystal before programming it for use. There is no definitive right or wrong method. Some may claim it won't reach its full potential if you don't cleanse it in a specific way, but that's not necessarily true. I believe that the best cleansing technique is the one that feels right for you. If it's not appropriately cleansed, you will likely notice it, and you may try several methods before finding the one that works best for you.

Cleansing techniques vary widely, and I've encountered several methods that people have found effective over the years. Here are a few that I've gathered you might find beneficial.

Running Water: This method involves holding the crystal under cold running water for a few minutes. Many believe water has cleansing properties, washing away any negative energy.

Salt Water: Another popular method is to soak crystals in a saltwater solution. However, be cautious, as salt can damage some crystals.

Sound: A singing bowl or a simple tuning fork can create vibrations that help cleanse crystals. The sound waves can help release stagnant or negative energy.

Smudging: This involves passing the crystal through the smoke of burning sage, cedar, or other cleansing herbs. The smoke is thought to purify the crystal and remove negativity.

Sunlight or Moonlight: Leaving your crystals out in the sunlight or moonlight can recharge and cleanse them naturally. Just be mindful of how long you leave them out since some crystals can fade in direct sunlight due to being chemically enhanced.

Burial: Placing the crystal in the earth for a few days can ground it and recharge its energy.

Visualisation: Some people prefer a more meditative approach, visualising light enveloping the crystal, cleansing it of any negativity.

Feel free to explore these methods and see which resonates most with you. The beauty of cleansing crystals is that it's a personal journey, and each technique can offer its own unique benefits. Don't hesitate to experiment and find what works best for you!

My favourite cleansing technique is to place the crystal on top of my Amethyst cluster. Amethyst is the only crystal that doesn't need cleansing, but if it makes you feel better about cleansing your Amethyst, do so.

It is best to cleanse your crystals every few months to clear their energy and program them again for your needs.

Programming Crystals

After cleansing a crystal, you can program it with your intentions or needs. To program a crystal, you blend its energy with your own and project this combined energy into the Universe to help manifest your desires using the crystal's energies.

For example, when we use Quartz for energy waves, we need to make all the necessary equipment adjustments for this to occur. This is somewhat what programming means; it is as simple as telling the crystal what you want: health, money, love, protection, etc.

Hold your recently cleansed crystal in your right hand (if you are left-handed, hold it in your left hand), make a fist, and meditate on the help you seek from the crystal. Imagine the manifestation of your goal. Like a movie in front of your eyes, see it manifesting, feel and live it, and it will happen.

Alternatively, rub both your hands together until they feel hot, then hold the crystal in both hands and experience the manifestation of your goal, as explained above. I have found that the electrical charges that emanate from my hands after I give them a good rub penetrate the crystal and merge its energy with mine.

Once you have programmed a crystal for a specific purpose, you should not allow anyone else to touch it, as this will send it off track. If you are out on the street and a stranger admires the beautiful Amethyst pendant around your neck, then reaches out and touches it before you have time to stop them, your crystal will be misguided.

The quickest way to cleanse a crystal is with saliva—moisten your index finger and rub it on it as quickly as possible. This way, you put your energies back into the crystal, then cleanse it and program it when you get home.

I would not be too concerned if your crystal encounters an immediate family member, as you are all on the same journey. But some people carry negative vibes, and you know who they are. If these people touch your crystal, cleanse it as soon as possible and guide it back to its original intent.

The Healing Shapes of Crystals

When crystals are identified on/in a mineral, they are in their *rough* state. Then, they are *polished*, *facetted*, or *tumbled* to give them shape and form. When this is done, they are converted to a varied collection of facetted beautiful pieces, each generating a different frequency for spiritual and physical healing according to its shape.

You have many options to choose from, and ultimately, the decision is yours. It might be challenging to pick just one because they are all beautifully crafted. It's like visiting a jewellery store filled with stunning cut-faceted pieces.

Some will have inclusions or phantoms inside the cut facetted crystal. These phantoms or inclusions are mesmerizing and form because of the precipitated growth of the actual crystals. You can have a Clear Quartz crystal; inside, you can see Loadstone or even Calcite.

No matter which crystal or how the inclusions or phantoms are formed, they all have a story to tell when you look deep within the actual faceted crystal. The inclusions could be identified differently by any individual. These can be anything from angel wings, fairies, or even lightning. Looking into a facetted crystal is like looking at tea leaves in a cup.

The shapes of the crystals are endless and more meaningful because you associate the inclusions with your needs, even your beliefs.

When picking a facetted crystal, you must already know why you are choosing one. Below, I have added some of the most popular ways people use facetted crystals in the home.

Rough - The crystal is in its original form, not touched by machinery and believed to be the better crystal for spiritual enlightenment and healing.

Obelisks - This crystal shape is used to bring down Universal energies and recollect past life experiences.

Tumble - This is the most popular shape. Rough crystals are placed inside a barrel with chemicals, abrasives and polishing compounds. It tumbles the rough pieces until the sharp edges are gone, and a polished and smooth finish is acquired. These crystals are mainly used after programming in little carry bags or placed in wallets, purses, handbags, or, most commonly, in a 'bra'.

Spheres - Spheres are communication balls. There are no points or facetted edges, so the direction goes to a more rounded place or gathering. It is said that if everyone had a crystal ball in their homes, our planet would start regenerating itself, so I have a Rose Quartz sphere that I fondly call Freda and many others. This way, I know I'm doing my bit; size is irrelevant.

Eggs—These have their own way of initiating energy. For healing, the egg-shaped crystal is easy to use and very versatile. The smaller end is directed at a specific part of the body. The end fits snugly in the palm of your hand. If reversed, it can be used as a massage tool.

Wands—These have a specific intent. As a rule, they have six facetted sides (hexagonal) and a smooth curved bottom. They are mainly used in magic, mostly by witches who do healing and encase them in copper wire to emanate more energy to their magical workings. Some of the ones I have seen are beautiful, not counting the work and precision that goes into their making.

Generators/Points—For most parts, generators have six facetted points (hexagonal), and the bottom is flat so that you can stand them. These can come in different sizes and widths. Generators are good for healing when pointed to the part of the body you wish to start healing on.

Double Terminated Generators—These are the same as Generators but have six more points on the other end. You can bring down Universal energies with one end and use the other to point to the area that needs healing.

Pyramids—This facetted shape is very popular and is believed to constantly bring down Universal healing according to its programming after cleaning. Pyramids are placed in popular places around the home where family and friends gather. They also bring wisdom, understanding, and communication.

Clusters—These come in any shape or mineral form and are usually of the same crystal structure. It is also known as a crystal family in a group of many points, possibly facing different directions or the same. A Clear Quartz cluster is one of the best crystals for protecting your home. The points face anywhere, and once programmed, they cover the entire house because the points are pointing in all different directions.

Geodes—There are Amethyst, Agates, and even Jasper geodes. These form from the outside in. A Geode is a surprise in the making; you don't know what's inside the sometimes-egg-shaped geode, which could be the size of your hand or be as tall as a person. Brazil has one of the biggest Geodes in the world; its many points are as long as an arm, some bigger than that. Once you open/ crack, let us say, an Amethyst, the middle is usually filled with many points, from deep to light purples.

Geodes bring harmony and peace to any home or room. They are not only a beautiful ornament, but they are also calming and resourceful in any home environment.

Scrying

Scrying, the predecessor of the Tarot, has been practised for centuries. Anything that shimmers or reflects can be used to glimpse the future. There are various methods for practising scrying. By focusing your mind, you can start to visualize mental images; however, the challenge lies in interpreting those images.

Unlike the Tarot, scrying does not offer as much guidance.

When you scry, you rely solely on your perception and intuition. One of the most respected and well-known scryers throughout history was Nostradamus. He was believed to have utilized crystals as one of many scrying methods of his time.

These days, the most popular way to scry is with a Clear Quartz sphere. The size is irrelevant; the mind expands the images shown before you. Many people keep the sphere wrapped around a white or purple silk scarf. Some feel that wrapping their sphere in black cloth protects it from negativity.

Before you start, cleanse your sphere like any other crystal. The way you cleanse your crystal sphere is up to you. Once done, you are ready to start. Sit in a quiet place, if you want to do it in the morning or at night, it is really up to you. It is essential to feel fantastic about what you will try to achieve and not just do it for the sake of doing it. Now, light a few candles and play relaxing background music.

Once done, you are ready to start.

Concentrate; focus solely on the sphere in front of you. It should feel like meditation. Sometimes, merely staring for a long time isn't the solution. Just relax and don't give up. Write down what you see and try to make sense of it; however, be aware that you might encounter nonsensical images. Embrace the pictures that emerge. The key to any psychic work is to meditate to calm the mind and connect with your intent.

Crystal Readings

I started reading crystals long before I realised I was doing it. When people select crystals, they often share their reasons for choosing a particular one. These reasons typically align with the crystals' meanings. This piqued my interest, and eventually, I realised I was being guided by spirit. As I grew more comfortable with this experience, I could often tell people why they had chosen a specific crystal.

For example, if someone selected an Amethyst, it usually indicated they were dealing with stress. If they chose a Rose Quartz, it often meant that a relationship was being tested and needed attention. When someone picked an Aventurine, it suggested they were struggling emotionally and having difficulty healing from past experiences that still haunted them. Lastly, if a person chose an Onyx, it indicated they were trapped in negative thoughts and needed to let go and embrace reason.

I don't believe in predicting the future with crystals; instead, I see their properties reflecting the needs and emotional state of the individual I'm connecting with during a reading. The crystals then begin their emotional journey to help heal that person, and I take a step back to witness their transformation as it unfolds.

I've had some clients tell me that the crystals didn't work. I explain that crystals function like herbal medicine and don't provide immediate results like conventional medications. If you want a quick fix, a pill might be the answer. However, when you're ready to explore other methods and embark on your spiritual journey, everything will start to make sense. Just give the crystals time; they are healing you from the inside out, slowly but surely.

I own ten crystals, which I keep in a small purple carry bag filled with lavender buds. Occasionally, I add a few drops of lavender and frankincense essential oils to keep the crystals fresh and energized after a reading.

There are many ways to conduct a crystal reading, with numerous combinations available. The greater the number of crystals, the more varieties and meanings arise. It's somewhat like playing the lottery—no two readings are the same. However, the one-crystal method is simple, straightforward, and an easy way to get started. As you gain experience and confidence, you'll find adding more crystals for specific questions easier by pulling extra ones as needed.

Practice is key. Begin with friends and family to build your comfort level before offering readings to others. You can also do readings for yourself as a weekly or daily guide.

While crystal divination, or what I sometimes refer to as crystal awareness, does not replace Tarot, Runes, or a reputable medium, it can serve as a valuable guide on your own or another person's spiritual journey, allowing love and universal light to enter your life.

The following are the crystals that are most trusted and best for starting your divination work. I would try to keep them all about the same size. It is best if they are tumbled so you can't feel the difference between the ten crystals when you pull one out of the pouch.

The recommended crystals are:
- Amethyst
- Aventurine
- Citrine
- Clear Quartz
- Hematite
- Onyx
- Red Jasper
- Rose Quartz
- Sodalite
- Tiger Eye

It is time to start once you have cleansed all your newfound divination crystals.

Programming your crystals: Rub your hands together to cause friction. Friction causes electrical charges and is the quickest and most effective way for your thoughts to penetrate the crystals. When you feel your hands are nice and hot, gather all the crystals and hold them in your hands. Visualise what you would like the crystal to foretell and foresee.

Where to keep your crystals?

May I suggest a velvet pouch. This way, you can pull a crystal without knowing which one you have picked, let the energy vibrations in your hands guide you, and choose the one that is most needed.

One crystal reading: This is when you pick only one crystal for a yes or no answer to your question, like: Put your hand inside the crystal pouch and ask a yes or a no question, like: How will my day be today or for the week? Then, pull one out; for example, if you picked a Rose Quartz, your day will be positive, and there is little you can't achieve. Carry it with you all day and reflect on its meaning and understanding. If it's a negative crystal, you will be aware that your day may not be as good as you'd hoped, but at least you will be mindful of it and prepared for anything that may turn up unexpectedly, positive or negative.

Amethyst – Positive

Amethyst wants to confirm that whatever your question was, it would be to your advantage, with new beginnings, a new job, and possibly a new course of study. Healing has started to work from within. Stress will finally be under control, knowing there are situations you have no control over.

Aventurine – Positive

When Aventurine is drawn, you will experience respite from negative energies and health issues. You will find that you can understand others without being judgmental. Relief from what has been bothering you is on the horizon. Expect new experiences to challenge you, but rest assured that these will lead to positive outcomes.

Citrine – Positive

Citrine encourages you to trust your instincts, as they are rarely wrong. Be prepared for a financial or emotional surprise. Pursuing a new course of study will be beneficial for your future finances. If you sense a situation is unfavourable, trust Citrine to warn and protect you. Luck is on your side when you draw Citrine; you can expect abundance in various aspects of your life. Remember to smile; good friends will soon reveal themselves.

Clear Quartz – Unsure.

Clear Quartz is telling you that the Universe is still undecided about the outcome, which can go either way depending on how you handle the situations that may arise during the day. So be prepared for the unexpected and handle karmic situations with control and assurance.

Hematite – Positive

Prepare for happiness for the remainder of this reading. You will find hope if you've felt lost, as things are starting to turn around for the better. Your dreams are within reach. Hematite encourages you to stay focused and never lose hope in your aspirations. There is no mountain you cannot climb and no sea you cannot swim in. If you want something to happen, the Universe is behind you 100%, so seize it and hold on to it; Hematite is a positive force in any reading outcome.

Onyx – Negative

Onyx indicates that your question may remain unanswered until you find a way to stop procrastinating and adopt a more positive outlook. Your tendency to change your mind frequently is hindering your spiritual growth. There are no right or wrong decisions, only choices that must be made to move forward. Stay focused, and Onyx will help dispel negativity, leading to a positive outcome in any given situation.

Red Jasper – Negative

Red Jasper serves as a warning; there may be emotional upsets, discord, and arguments when this crystal is drawn. It's essential to stop and think before you act; many issues can be prevented by careful consideration.

Red Jasper gives you the courage to handle unwanted situations and explore new horizons or job opportunities. Remember, just because Red Jasper appears on the negative side of a question, it doesn't signal disaster. Instead, if appropriately managed, it can transform a negative situation into a positive one.

Rose Quartz – Positive.

Rose Quartz wants you to know that your doubts are justified, but have faith in who you are, as there is no reason for a negative outcome. Relationships are tested, but communication is free from petty arguments. If you are looking for that new love, don't despair; it is coming sooner than you think, and if you still haven't found it, more work needs to be done on loving who you are so you can attract that special person in your life.

Sodalite – Negative

Sodalite can warn against unfavourable situations and keep you on your toes for whatever comes your way, like an unpleasant situation at work, an argument with a friend or a partner, or discord with children. Still, whatever it may bring, Sodalite can work through negative situations with easy communicative persuasion. If the question concerns a health issue, be assured that whatever ails you, Sodalite will have the power to pacify and direct you to the proper channels to heal and overcome it, so don't despair.

Tiger Eye – Negative

Tiger Eye warns that what you thought was beneficial may not be. There are negative forces at work, and it may be necessary to distance yourself from them; you could be your worst enemy now. Someone might blame you for a dispute that benefits them. Trust that Tiger Eye is absorbing all the negativity around you while reminding you to remain positive, as changes are coming.

Initiating A New Way of Life

Many people ask me if it is bad luck to give crystals as gifts. Of course not! In fact, when a crystal is given to someone with love and understanding, it means more than if they had bought it for themselves. The crystal becomes infused with the idea that someone appreciates its unique qualities and wishes to share its benefits with a friend.

An intuitive person can select the appropriate crystal based on its colour, shape, and properties or use the crystal numerology chart in this book

It's essential never to take a crystal that does not belong to you, as this can result in bad karma. However, if you find a crystal abandoned in an outdoor space, it's a sign from the Universe that it wants you to have it; you should consider it yours. If you lose a crystal, it means its mission with you has ended. The Universe has made this happen because someone else needs it more than you do, and it's time for you to move on.

If a crystal breaks, it signifies that it has absorbed negativity on your behalf to protect you from harm. In this case, it's best to bury the broken crystal in the ground, along with the negativity it has taken on, and never wear it again.

Remember that crystals have existed since the beginning of time and have been bestowed upon us by Mother Nature, the earth element, and the crystal guardians of the Universe. Crystals have a wide range of influences, but they are generally powerful protective and healing talismans that can transform your life in any way you desire—provided you are open to change.

All crystals are precious and beautiful. They have supported our ancestors spiritually and physically for centuries. Once you incorporate them into your life, you will understand and appreciate the love crystals can bring. In return, each crystal offers you a little gift in return.

Crystals A-Z

Agate

Colour
Various true colours: Blue, grey-white,
rust, light to dark brown orange

Spiritual Influence

Agate has a healing, loving vibration that promotes happiness and inner peace. It protects against negative thoughts and emotions and encourages a kindly, easy-going nature in its wearer. It brings inspiration and luck and promotes fidelity between couples.

Blue Lace Agate is associated with the water element. It enhances creative expression and promotes a contented mind. Blue Lace Agate is used in the home to deter evil spirits or harmful energy. If there have been tensions or arguments between household members, it can help to calm loved ones' bad tempers.

Dendritic Agate is known for its protective power. If you are an intrepid traveller who enjoys taking risks, carry a piece of Dendritic Agate; it will protect you from physical danger and provide you with the energy and courage you need to move through obstacles easily.

Traditionally, it was used in healing rituals and spells to enhance fertility.

During stressful periods, wear Blue Lace Agate to promote relaxation and balance.

Moss Agate is a crystal of courage and abundance. It is worn to attract love, happiness, health, and good fortune and is believed to assist in acquiring wealth. Moss agate has grounding vibrations and helps you attune to the earth. It shields against dark spells by destructive individuals and helps alleviate anger.

Physical Influence

Agate is a soothing crystal that calms and rejuvenates the body. It restores physical energy when you are feeling run down and assists with the healing of minor ailments. It speeds up the healing of fractures and the recovery after a traumatic illness. It also promotes strength and longevity.

Dendritic Agate strengthens eyesight and sharpens the mind.

Alexandrite

Colour
Bluish-green and pink under lights

Spiritual Influence

Alexandrite can influence people with addictive personalities. It aids with creativity, making it excellent for writers, artists, actors, and anyone in the arts. It creates expression of the self and a vision of what can be. If placed under a pillow, Alexandrite is an excellent crystal for interpreting lucid dreams.

Physical Influence

Alexandrite works well with all the vital organs, making it an excellent crystal for liver, pancreas, spleen, and heart ailments.

It is also a wonderful crystal for testicular cancer.

Amazonite

Colour
Bluish-green

Spiritual Influence

Amazonite amplifies your personality and encourages you to recognise your strengths.

If you desire to change but feel fearful about moving forward, wear Amazonite to help you find and follow your path in life. It lets you let go of beliefs and habits that inhibit your potential. It also fortifies the body's energy currents, promoting spiritual healing and growth.

Amazonite is ideal for artists, writers, and musicians, as it enhances the flow of creative expression.

When worn, amazonite encourages an amiable and easy-going disposition. It stimulates mental processes and promotes rational thinking, which is beneficial for study and emergency situations.

Physical Influence

Amazonite is a cooling, soothing crystal that calms the nerves and mind.

Amazonite is a strengthening and fortifying crystal that is good for bones. It is helpful for those prone to osteoporosis and/or arthritis, as it helps prevent calcium deficiency.

Amber (Resin)

Colour

Honey-yellow

Spiritual Influence

Amber is not a crystal but a fossilised resin from cone-bearing trees. It often contains fragments from insects and plants and is believed to be full of healing life forces.

When worn, Amber brings luck and personal magnetism and protects against negativity from others. It is often used in love-attracting spells and heals the body spiritually.

Amber can also amplify your intuition or "gut feeling". It can help restore a positive outlook after strife or disappointment.

Amber enhances natural beauty and allure. If you wear a string of amber beads around your neck, the radiant beauty within you will shine out and attract those around you.

Physical Influence

Because amber is such an ancient substance, it is associated with strength and longevity. It has long been recognised as a healing crystal and is used to assist in the treatment of ulcers, sore throats, and thyroid problems. It also helps to strengthen the digestive system. Amber is also an excellent tool for teething in a necklace form.

Amethyst

Colour
Light to dark violet

Spiritual Influence

Amethyst has a calming, peaceful vibration. It is used to cleanse the aura. It aids in clearing blockages with spiritual clarity.

Wearing an Amethyst will give you a sense of inner peace and understanding if you are prone to the ills of everyday stressors. It also encourages emotional flexibility, helping you to accept endings and new beginnings. Carry an Amethyst crystal when making a difficult decision about a heart-related matter or when you need to come to terms with the death of a loved one.

Amethyst is an excellent meditation tool. Holding a piece in your hand will help you tune in to insight from a deeper source. It is particularly ideal for those with violent tendencies, as it helps to calm inner anger and magnifies the consciousness of the higher self.

Physical Influence

Amethyst is helpful for insomniacs or those prone to nightmares. When placed beneath the pillow, it ensures a restful sleep.

A healing crystal, Amethyst, can help with headaches and back pain. It is also helpful for those with cancer or chronic health conditions.

Amethyst has long been used for overcoming addictions, particularly alcoholism. When held, it helps to draw pain, anger and sorrow from the body.

Ametrine

Colour
Purple with Yellow inclusions

Spiritual Influence

Ametrine is an Amethyst and Citrine blend. Some pieces have more Amethyst than Citrine. Ametrine has the same polarities as Amethyst.

Ametrine is warm and mysterious. It awakens the senses and tunes in to past lives, allowing you to understand better your soul's journey through your Akashic records, the imprint of your past lives.

Physical Influences

Ametrine calms GRD syndrome. It aids with indigestion and digestion, minimising stomach ulcers and kidney and liver disease.

Apache Tear

Colour

Dark brown to black

Spiritual Influence

Apache Tear is an uplifting crystal useful in times of grief and sorrow. Legend has it that if you carry an Apache Tear, you will never need to cry again because it will act as a substitute for yours.

Often called "the positive crystal", an Apache Tear can be worn to bring luck and promote an optimistic outlook on life. It can help you see the bright side of even the most difficult issues.

Apache Tear also protects against danger and negative magic. Wear it during strife to ensure that those who try to take advantage of you fail.

Physical Influence

Apache Tear strengthens the skeletal structure and is suitable for spinal problems. It is also an excellent crystal for ex-intravenous drug users, fortifying the veins and helping to restore their original flexibility.

Apache Tear promotes physical and emotional balance and is helpful for those prone to seizures.

Apatite

Colour
Brownish-red, bluish-green, red,
violet, white or yellowish green

Spiritual Influence

Apatite stimulates the intellect and enhances creativity. For this reason, it is an excellent crystal for study and artistic pursuits such as writing, designing, painting and playing music.

A cleansing crystal, Apatite helps to release congestion from the Chakras. It is also helpful for meditation, promoting clarity and focus.

Apatite's influence is inspirational and healing. Wear or carry it to awaken your true feelings and help you resolve childhood emotional traumas. Apatite encourages your higher self to evolve to your fullest potential.

Physical Influence

Apatite can help those with mental illness by dispelling confusion. It also strengthens the body's major organs, reducing swelling in the glands.

Apophyllite

Colour
Pearly-white, clear with white streaks

Spiritual Influence

Apophyllite promotes mental clarity and expands psychic awareness. It is used in meditation to tap into the spiritual realm and aid communication with the fairy kingdom. It also helps facilitate astral travel.

If confused, Apophyllite will help you listen to your inner self and act upon your intuitive knowing. When worn or carried, Apophyllite allows you to see through fraudulence and deception and recognise the truth of any situation.

Physical Influence

Apophyllite stimulates the pineal gland and helps break up energy blockages in the brain. It can also help relieve sinus problems and conjunctivitis. Apophyllite can also soothe tired, aching feet when placed in a warm footbath.

Aquamarine

Colour
Bluish-green, light blue

Spiritual Influence

Aquamarine has a peaceful vibration and engenders mental alertness, purification, emotional balance, and courage. It enhances personal relationships by giving its wearer a sense of responsibility towards others and promoting harmonious interactions. It makes adults responsible for their actions.

Like Amethyst, Aquamarine calms the mind and strengthens mental clarity. It is an excellent crystal for writers and poets, as it opens the mind to higher levels of inspiration and enhances fluent expression.

Aquamarine is often used in divination and magic because it purifies energy and sharpens psychic perception. It has also been known to activate past-life memories.

Wear or carry Aquamarine to banish fears and phobias.

Because Aquamarine is a potent purifier, it is helpful for energetic cleansing. Rub the crystal over your body to remove negativity or place it in the bathtub when bathing.

Physical Influence

Aquamarine is a soothing crystal that can help relieve a toothache. It also reduces fluid retention and improves vision and general health. It is used to assist in treating ailments affecting the stomach, throat, and jaw. It also relieves swelling due to menstruation.

Aventurine

Colour
Light to dark green with metallic flecks

Spiritual Influence

Aventurine is a healing crystal that produces a deep tranquillity when held or worn. Like many green crystals, it calms troubled thoughts and turbulent emotions.

Babies benefit from this crystal to help resolve past-life issues. The healing process can begin by placing an Aventurine crystal in a blue sock above the cot.

As a talisman, Aventurine is carried to attract money. It also brings thrills and good fortune in love.

Aventurine aligns emotions with the intellect, promoting clear perception. It endows its wearer with leadership qualities and encourages independence and originality.

Aventurine also stimulates creativity. It brings you in touch with your masculine and feminine sides.

If you are having trouble sleeping, hold a piece of Aventurine; within minutes, your mind will quieten, and you will slip into a deep slumber.

Physical Influence

Aventurine expands the lungs and increases breathing ease. It is also helpful in relieving muscular pain and speeding the healing process.

A potent restorative, Aventurine heals the body on a mental, emotional, and spiritual level. It also balances the pituitary gland.

I have also found that Aventurine is a great healing tool for animals. I have often used this with healing on my own and my friends' animals. It also aids bone fractures and torn muscles in our four-legged friends,

Azurite

Colour

Deep blue

Spiritual Influence

Azurite amplifies psychic perception, insight, and intuition. It is also helpful for magical work, as it acts as a messenger between you, your spirit guides and the guardians of the Universe.

Azurite is also an ideal meditation tool because it calms mental activity and clears the mind of confusion.

Physical Influence

Azurite promotes growth in children and stimulates energy flow in the nervous system. It is also helpful for anxiety sufferers, as it lessens pressure in the chest.

Azurite With Malachite

Colour

Blue and green

Spiritual Influence

Azurite-Malachite stimulates psychism and promotes emotional stability. It also strengthens the mind, improving memory and intellectual dexterity.

When carried or worn, Azurite-Malachite will calm you down, even when emotional turmoil surrounds you. It helps you rise above negativity and bestows intuitive understanding and compassion.

Azurite-Malachite is also excellent for meditation because it provides focus. It helps you turn off the chatter of the conscious mind so that you can delve into the depths of your inner self.

Physical Influence

Azurite-Malachite aids detoxification and is helpful for those suffering from asthma, ulcers, and circulatory problems. It is also beneficial for insomniacs. Placing a crystal beneath your pillow will improve your sleeping patterns and allow you to interpret your dreams more easily.

Bloodstone

Colour
Dark to dull green with red flecks

Spiritual Influence

Bloodstone helps balance extreme moods and promotes a constructive mindset. It also brings luck and courage, making it easier for shy individuals to attract friends.

If you're an actor, singer, or dancer looking for new job opportunities, wearing or carrying a Bloodstone can boost your self-confidence and creative abilities.

In ancient times, Bloodstone was worn to protect against the "evil eye." It was also utilised in court cases to help ensure victory in legal battles.

Physical Influence

Traditionally, Bloodstone was used in ancient times to stop bleeding. Soldiers carried it as a first aid tool. Pregnant women wore it to prevent miscarriage and ease childbirth.

Today, Bloodstone's cooling influence is used to reduce fevers. It is worn as a general healing talisman and to purify the blood.

Blue Quartz

Colour
Dull blue

Spiritual Influence

Blue Quartz is associated with the ocean and promotes peace and tranquillity. It also increases psychism and helps you confront and release your emotional fears.

When worn around the neck, Blue Quartz activates the throat Chakra and encourages speaking one's mind without hurting others. For this reason, it is ideal for introverts and those who tend to internalise their feelings.

Physical Influence

Blue Quartz calms chronic health conditions. It also assists in relieving any throat ailment.

Calcite

Colour
Clear blue, green, pink, orange or yellow

Spiritual Influence

Calcite amplifies energy and stimulates the Chakras, activating all the colours of the rainbow. It also supports clear communication during difficult interactions.

Clear Calcite. It is suitable for focusing the mind and is an excellent meditation tool.

Blue Calcite. It is used for spiritual healing and purification.

Green Calcite. It is suitable for grounding and emotional balance and is also used in prosperity rituals.

Pink Calcite. It is a calming crystal that promotes love and peace.

Yellow Calcite. It is used to assist astral travel and enhance channelling abilities.

Physical Influence

Calcite improves calcium intake in the bones and strengthens the liver and kidneys.

Orange Calcite, which is ruled by the sun and associated with the fire element, is held or worn to increase energy levels and regenerate the body after a period of illness or fatigue.

Carnelian Agate

Colour
Orange, red or reddish-brown

Spiritual Influence

Carnelian protects against negativity and harmful magic. Wearing this crystal is akin to covering your body in invisible armour.

If you feel trapped by obstacles and difficulties, Carnelian encourages you to transform negative thinking into supportive behaviour patterns.

Carnelian is also a powerful tool for healing a broken heart and releasing sorrow after disappointment in love. Wear or carry this crystal when you need more courage and self-confidence.

Carnelian increases sexual energy and will help stimulate you to communicate your sexual and emotional needs. Wearing Carnelian can take a relationship or love interest to new heights of passion!

Physical Influence

Carnelian strengthens the female reproductive system and is a general health talisman. Wear or carry Carnelian in spring to protect against allergens. When you have a cold, place a piece of Carnelian under your pillow to assist with ease of breathing.

Cat's Eye

Colour
Grey to green to yellow, also white,
red, blue, brown, or black

Spiritual Influence

Cat's Eye is a powerful crystal for dispelling negativity from others. It protects the wearer from bad luck while attracting positive energy from those around them, allowing for a greater appreciation of life's offerings. This crystal can be used in spells to enhance the desired outcomes and serves as a protective shield against hostile occult forces directed at you. Additionally, Cat's Eye is excellent for tuning into other people's energies during a spiritual reading.

Physical Influence

Cat's Eye can help to relieve physical illnesses, such as headaches or stress, that we inflict upon ourselves.

Celestine

Colour

Sky Blue

Spiritual Influence

If you are starting on your spiritual journey, Celestine is an excellent crystal to use. When carried, it brings peace and love to the self until there is enough love within to attract the love of your life. It expresses truth and understanding of higher spiritual awareness.

It is relaxing and calming, and teaches you to reason with others. It allows you to express how you feel in ways that are not offensive or disturbing, but allow you to make your point. It awakens personal awareness of creativity.

Celestine works with the power of Angels. Carry it with you if you need protection, and the Angels will hear the vibrations and let you know they heard you. While meditating, Celestine will take you to places you have never known that would leave you breathless and wanting more.

Physical Influence

Celestine aids sore throats and sores due to diabetes and helps with pain management for those who suffer from chronic pain, such as backaches, headaches, or joint pain.

Charoite

Colour

Purple and Pink

Spiritual Influence

Charoite helps you understand others, their actions, and why they do them. It enables you to grasp the technology of the modern age and assimilate the advancements without confusion, but with understanding.

Charoite processes life lessons that we have yet to learn. It clears space for new experiences and allows people to be more open to the world and its changes and acceptance. Charoite is the crystal you would use if you wanted to be in the right place at the right time.

Physical Influence

Carry a Charoite to prevent cataracts and eye-related problems. It aids in absorbing daily toxins, understanding the pancreas, and helps break down carbohydrates. Runners carry this crystal to maintain a healthy heart rate while exercising.

Chalcopyrite

Colour
Greenish black with brassy yellow streaks

Spiritual Influence

Chalcopyrite stimulates the flow of energy throughout the body. It is a powerful tool for removing energy blockages and revitalising the mind and body.

A crystal of transformation, Chalcopyrite helps you peel back the "self" layers that hide the real you. This crystal is helpful to wear when trying to find lost objects around the house.

Those who work with terminally ill patients often wear it to help them come to terms with death and deal with others' pain.

Physical Influence

Chalcopyrite is a healing crystal that benefits the nervous system and body organs. It also stimulates hair growth and reduces joint inflammation.

Chrysocolla

Colour
Light green with bluish streaks

Spiritual Influence

Chrysocolla is an ideal crystal for the home or workplace, as it purifies a room's energy. It is often referred to as "the peacemaker," as it calms emotions and promotes easy communication and understanding.

Chrysocolla can help bring a new romantic relationship into your life when worn. If you are having trouble deciding whether a potential partner suits you, this crystal will aid you with the process.

Chrysocolla is also helpful because it heightens your capacity to be discerning.

Physical Influence

Chrysocolla promotes physical strength and balance. It is an excellent crystal for those with diabetes, as it helps to regulate blood sugar levels.

Chrysoprase

Colour
Emerald to apple green

Spiritual Influence

Chrysoprase is a crystal of pure joy. It endows its wearer with grace and compassion and helps to balance the energies of the emotional, mental, and physical bodies.

Chrysoprase is a powerful protector who repels negativity, stress, tension, and jealousy. This crystal is worn to promote friendship and success in new ventures.

Chrysoprase is also used to enhance fertility. If you have been trying to conceive a child without success, try wearing Chrysoprase and get your partner to wear it, to even the odds.

If you are accident-prone, wearing Chrysoprase can help protect you from everyday mishaps and minor accidents.

Physical Influence

A healing crystal, Chrysoprase, is worn or carried to improve eyesight, stabilise blood pressure, and strengthen the female reproductive system.

Citrine

Colour
Light to Golden yellow

Spiritual Influence

Citrine lifts your spirits and evokes optimism. It can give hope when you are despondent and help you derive pleasure and happiness from the simple things in life, such as friends, food, work, and nature. It increases intuitive perception.

Citrine is a crystal of luck and abundance used in rituals to increase cash flow. Wear or carry it when beginning a new relationship or business venture. Citrine is a good crystal to have when in a course of study or learning, and should be worn. Children benefit from this crystal if placed in a school pencil case for concentration.

Physical Influence

Citrine is helpful for those with thyroid problems, ulcers, and degenerative disease. It also aids digestion.

Clear Quartz

Colour
Clear or dull white

Spiritual Influence

Clear Quartz purifies and amplifies energy and has multiple uses and purposes. Clear Quartz crystal points are worn, carried, or placed in the home to increase psychic ability and dispel negativity. They can also help you access information in your unconscious mind and facilitate communication with your spirit guides.

As an effective energy conductor, Clear Quartz crystal points are utilised in magic to enhance their power. Use a crystal wand to amplify your intent when performing a spell or ritual.

Clear Quartz also promotes mental clarity and focus. If you are confused or unsure about an appropriate course of action, meditating with Clear Quartz can help you reach a pertinent resolution.

To strengthen the power of your Clear Quartz crystal, place it under the light of a full moon. It can help you come to terms with your sexuality and determine your sexual preference. It aids in boosting the mind to retain written matter when studying.

Physical Influence

Clear Quartz is an all-round healing crystal. It is worn or carried to help detoxify the body and assist recovery from illness.

Shamans and energy healers use crystal points to remove energy blockages in diseased body areas. Clear Quartz crystals are added to herbal and flower essences and elixirs to enhance their effectiveness.

Clear Quartz is the ultimate healer.

Copal (Resin)

Colour
Yellow or Red-Brown

Spiritual Influence

Copal unblocks projections to the Universe from your mind's eye. Its yellow and sometimes red-brown colours can contact other realms in the Universe and playback information from higher beings, be they spirits or aliens. It is an excellent crystal for meditation and the acquisition of personal enlightenment.

Physical Influence

Copal has healing qualities for hysterectomy patients, ovarian tumours, and cervical dysplasia. It is also great for women while they are giving birth and for those who are trying to get pregnant.

Coral (Shell)

Colour

A range of many colours

Spiritual Influence

Even though coral falls under the shell category, it comes from the ocean, which is as old as time itself. Its spiritual influence is endless, and of course, it is a gift from the element of water that deals with every single one of our emotions. It seems many of us cry in the shower, so maybe keep it in the bathroom to help you shed the emotions that haunt you, to help release them.

Physical Influence

The best physical influence would be on the pituitary gland. During stressful and emotional times, the pituitary gland expands and wreaks havoc with the endocrine system, which can cause headaches and visual impairment. Women can even lactate at this time as prolactin levels escalate above the normal range.

Diamond

Colour

Clear, sometimes with a blue, green, yellow, pink, or dark hue

Spiritual Influence

Although Diamonds are best known for their dazzling beauty and high price tag, they also have spiritual value. They are practical meditation tools, as they amplify psychic receptivity and allow you to reach higher levels of consciousness.

When worn, Diamonds provide inner spiritual strength and courage. They also protect against quarrels and emotional strain.

Traditionally, the groom gave Diamonds to the bride to ensure fidelity in marriage. Today, Diamonds are the most popular crystal used in engagement rings.

Physical Influence

When worn or carried, Diamonds increase physical strength. They also help improve eyesight, relieve muscular spasms, and alleviate problems associated with diabetes.

Emerald

Colour
Emerald green

Spiritual Influence

Emeralds are associated with love, happiness, and relaxation. It also sharpens the intellect and stimulates psychism.

Often called "the kind crystal", Emerald bestows its wearer with compassion and sensitivity. It relieves emotional turmoil and promotes a greater understanding of the inner self.

If you wish to draw more love into your life, program an Emerald with your intent and always carry it with you. Emeralds are also used in rituals to attract money and abundance.

Physical Influence

Emeralds have a soothing, healing vibration. They are used to strengthen eyesight and relieve tired, sore eyes. This crystal regulates diabetes in sufferers.

Fluorite

Colour
Streaks of blue, green, red and violet

Spiritual Influence

Fluorite stabilises the mind and facilitates objectivity. It is an excellent crystal to wear for meditation and concentration because it heightens clarity and focus. It is also ideal for divination because it prevents self-delusion and assists in perceiving the truth of a given situation.

If your emotions are clouding your thoughts or you are in turmoil, wear Fluorite to help you detach and acquire a more accurate perspective on the issue that is bothering you.

Fluorite dispels feelings of anger, fear, and depression and balances the conscious mind.

Physical Influence

Fluorite strengthens bones and teeth and benefits people with rheumatoid arthritis. It can assist in the treatment of depression and other mental illnesses. Because it stimulates the intellect and increases mental powers, it is also ideal for people who have suffered strokes.

Garnet

Colour

Dark red

Spiritual Influence

A Garnet is a protective crystal that dispels negativity from all the Chakras and fortifies the aura. Known as 'the warrior crystal', it will always be your fighting spirit.

Travellers often wear it to repel harmful influences.

Garnets are also used for past-life regression because they promote mental fortitude. They calm anger, promote patience and responsibility, and encourage love and compassion for oneself.

Garnets also enhance physical vitality and endurance. Wear or carry a crystal when you need extra energy for exercise, study, or intensive ritual work.

Physical Influence

Often called "the crystal of health," garnets strengthen all the organs of the body, particularly the heart and skin.

They also regulate the blood.

Hematite

Colour
Metallic grey

Spiritual Influence

Hematite is a grounding crystal that radiates "kind love". It promotes harmony and connection to the earth. If you are nervous, jumpy, or highly strung, wearing hematite will help you operate in a state of balance and grace. It is also suitable for mathematical endeavours.

Hematite is also helpful in overcoming fear and increasing courage and strength. Negative expectations will melt away when you are infused with the energy of this crystal. It enables you to see all sides of a situation.

Hematite is suitable for older people as it strengthens memory.

Physical Influence

Hematite assists oxygen circulation throughout the body and is excellent for the heart and blood. Since ancient times, it has been used to balance and cleanse the physical body and to drive off illness.

Hematite can effectively relieve headaches when placed on the skin over the temples or at the base of the skull.

Howlite

Colour
White with grey lines

Spiritual Influence

Howlite has a peaceful, relaxing vibration and facilitates open, honest communication and emotional expression.

Often called "the tranquillity crystal, "Howlite alleviates fear, stress, pain, and rage and promotes patience and rational thinking. It confers empathy and discernment in challenging situations and encourages you to behave subtly and tactfully.

Howlite is also a crystal of ambition and determination. It will give you the certainty of purpose to achieve your goals successfully.

Physical Influence

Because of its high calcium content, Howlite is believed to benefit pregnant women and nursing mothers. It is also worn to strengthen teeth, bones, and other body tissues.

Iolite

Colour
Blue – Violet

Spiritual Influence

Iolite works well with psychics, mediums, and tarot readers. It helps them connect with their spiritual guides for past, present, and future information. It also assists the hypnotist in getting through to his subject to enhance the desired hypnotic state.

Physical Influence

Excellent for everyday use, with little memory lost, like where I put the car keys or what I was supposed to get in the supermarket. Iolite aids the intake of blue rays and may assist people undergoing radioactive therapy.

Jade

Colour

Opaque, pale to dark green

(lavender, red, yellow, and black)

Spiritual Influence

Jade is a crystal of luck, love, courage, and wisdom. It confers a feeling of self-assuredness and contentment and helps you realise your potential and purpose.

Lavender - Peace and harmony
Red - Strength and vitality
Yellow - Leaning and intuition
Black - Protection and negativity

Since ancient times, the Chinese have exchanged Jade jewellery to strengthen lovers' bonds and ensure marriage fidelity. When worn, carried, or placed in the home, Jade encourages one to release the self-imposed limitations that stand in the way of one's desires.

Jade also enhances the intellect and the attainment of knowledge. It brings clarity when there is confusion and restores hope when there is doubt.

When placed under your pillow for sleep, Jade can assist you in recalling and interpreting your dreams.

Jade protects against verbal abuse and is especially ideal for women who are subject to it from their partners, boyfriends, parents, and so-called friends.

Physical Influence

Jade's soothing green colour reflects its healing vibrations. It strengthens the body's healing ability and helps release suppressed disease-associated emotions.

Jade is particularly beneficial for the heart and digestive system. In China, it is worn to promote longevity.

Jade also strengthens the body's filtration system and protects against damage from substance abuse.

Jasper (Red)

Colour

Burnt red

Spiritual Influence

Red Jasper is a protective and grounding crystal. It increases awareness of your connection to the Earth and repels negative energy and evil. It also strengthens the power of your intent and is used in rituals to attract material abundance.

It is helpful to wear or carry a Red Jasper when seeking employment. It promotes mental balance and confidence, enabling you to overcome doubts, fears, and illusions. It also strengthens the power of your intent.

A stabilising crystal, Red Jasper balances the auric field and eases the pain associated with emotional problems.

Physical Influence

Red Jasper purifies the blood and revitalises the brain, improving mental acuity. Its energy rejuvenates and strengthens the body.

In ancient times, Red Jasper was used to reduce fevers and the pain of childbirth. It also enhances hormone balance and tissue growth and repair.

Red Jasper enhances fertility and prevents setbacks in physical disorders.

Jet (Wood Fossilised)

Colour
Black

Spiritual Influence

It helps nourish the Chakras. Jet is a positive crystal for those negative souls who see nothing but their own point of view. Jet can also keep finances healthy in business and during the launch of new products.

Physical Influence

Jet is suitable for treating a cold or flu if placed in a handkerchief with a few leaves of Eucalyptus. To prevent headaches, place the Jet under your pillow every night. It is an excellent crystal for those suffering from depression; it helps them see the light at the end of the tunnel.

Kunzite

Colour

Light blue, light pink, or violet

Spiritual Influence

Kunzite has a powerful, loving energy. Wearing or carrying this crystal stimulates loving thoughts and feelings, enhancing self-esteem.

Kunzite is a protective crystal useful for meditation and communicating with the spirit world. It strengthens the aura, repels negative energy, and promotes spiritual awareness and growth.

Kunzite also confers confidence and bestows inner freedom. Wear this crystal to protect yourself from disturbing emotions and negativity.

Physical Influence

Kunzite has a high lithium content and is ideal for those with manic depression, eating disorders, or addictions.

A purifying crystal, Kunzite also assists in treating kidney stones, blood disorders, heart conditions, and migraine headaches.

Labradorite

Colour
Peacock blue, green, Gold, and rust

Spiritual Influence

Labradorite is one of the nicest and most mesmerising crystals. It does not matter how you hold it; rainbows of infinite colours and shapes follow each moment. Labradorite helps to strengthen your intuition and help you make decisions that are strong for your well-being. It gives you courage to pursue new endeavours and to follow them through.

Physical Influence

Excellent for people with addictions. If placed under a pillow it will aid the flow of brain waves. This crystal regulates menstrual cycle.

Lapis Lazuli

Colour

Deep blue to bluish green with flecks of Golden Pyrite and calcite

Spiritual Influence

Lapis Lazuli opens the third eye and enhances psychic perception. It promotes tranquillity and spiritual clarity and helps one attune to the energies surrounding the self.

When you place a Lapis Lazuli on your skin, it has a cooling, soothing effect. It can turn anger and rage into feelings of peace and love, stimulating spiritual awareness.

Lapis Lazuli also gives you the courage to speak your truth. It is a helpful crystal when dealing with love and relationship issues because it helps you understand your true feelings and instinctively "know" what is right for you.

Physical Influence

Lapis Lazuli is used for health, growth, and physical protection. When worn often, it strengthens the immune system and cleanses the body of toxins. It also helps to relieve fevers and muscular tension caused by anxiety.

Lazurite

Colour

Blue

Spiritual Influence

Lazurite promotes inner peace for the wearer, allowing the soul to find calmness and reflect on its original intentions. If you're struggling to decide, hold a Lazurite crystal in your hands, and within a few days, clarity will come, helping you to reach a conclusion.

Physical Influence

Because of its soothing, deep blue colour, Lazurite calms all ailments, including joint inflammations, aches, and other physical strains.

Lepidolite

Colour
Violet, lilac, pale red, grey

Spiritual Influence

Lepidolite is rich in lithium, so it has a calming energy that relaxes and sedates its wearer. It balances the energies of the mental and emotional bodies and confers hope and love.

If you are depressed or angry, Lepidolite will help you ride the storms of life. It is beneficial during times of transition because it enables you to let go of fear and to have faith in your ability to handle change.

Lepidolite is also a spiritual crystal that enhances psychic ability.

Physical Influence

Lepidolite relieves insomnia and dissipates anxiety and stress. Because it calms the mind, it is helpful for those with manic depression and addictions.

Lepidolite is good for the heart and alleviates muscle tension.

Loadstone

Colour

Grey

Spiritual Influence

When all financial expectations are gone, Loadstone can come to the rescue. It's such a positive crystal, even if its colour does not indicate it. When placed inside your wallet, it brings money in. It aids in keeping things in perspective without interfering with others. It finds hope when there is none around.

Physical Influence

It is excellent to use in healing rituals as it pulls sickness from the body like a magnet.

Malachite

Colour

Deep emerald to light green with bands of very light green to white

Spiritual Influence

Malachite promotes emotional balance and transformation. It can help you understand and clear past negative behaviour patterns and assist you in finding your true path in life.

A crystal of peace and tranquillity, Malachite opens the heart and increases one's ability to love. It is worn to attract love.

Malachite has long been a traveller's talisman, as it protects against danger and prevents falls.

Physical Influence

Malachite is a powerful healer. It strengthens the eyes and immune system and helps relieve asthma and arthritis. It also relaxes the nervous system and can reveal the underlying emotional factors that may be causing illness.

Malachite is beneficial for chemotherapy patients. It also helps protect against radiation's effects, promoting tissue regeneration.

Moldavite

Colour
Dark to light green

Spiritual Influence

Moldavite holds messages from other worlds and different planes of existence. It facilitates communication with the spirit world, helping to translate messages and lessons for us to learn. Additionally, it amplifies the process of channelling. This crystal is excellent for meditating on the outcome of a situation.

Physical Influence

Moldavite is a crystal used by many for the heart and conditions related to surgery for its healing powers.

Moonstone

Colour
Pearly-white, sometimes with
a soft pink, blue or yellow hue

Spiritual Influence

Moonstone stimulates the feminine or yin side of your nature, promoting gentleness, compassion, and love. As the sacred crystal of the Moon Goddess, it has a protective energy, particularly when swimming or travelling over water. It also enhances sensitivity and intuitive perception.

Moonstone alleviates anxiety and stress from all the water signs and helps you connect with your true feelings. It cleanses negative energy from all the Chakras, bringing confidence, composure, joy, and happiness.

Wearing a Moonstone during times of transition is helpful, as it encourages you to move with the ebb and flow of life. It assists you in handling difficult situations with diplomacy. It is also a crystal of wish-fulfilment, useful for new beginnings.

Physical Influence

Moonstone soothes pain and regenerates the organs and tissues of the body. It is beneficial for women because it helps maintain hormonal balance and enhances the health of the reproductive system. When worn, it eases childbirth.

Obsidian and Snowflake Obsidian

Colour
Black or black with white flecks

Spiritual Influence

Obsidian is a grounding, protective crystal that protects against emotional abuse. When worn, it dissipates negativity and stress and purifies energy.

Obsidian helps you connect to what is usually hidden in your nature and accentuates your strengths. It is believed to broaden your horizons and stimulate the desire to travel.

A crystal of achievement, Obsidian is ideal for those who wish to obtain prosperity. It provides the determination to move through obstacles and the confidence to succeed.

Obsidian was used to make knives, arrowheads, and other sharp tools in ancient times.

Physical Influence

Because of its strength and density, When worn, it enhances the strength of bones and veins and relaxes tired eyes.

Obsidian also has a detoxifying and regenerating influence. It is ideal for those susceptible to environmental pollutants and emotional strain. It improves the condition of the skin to alleviate acne.

Onyx

Colour

Black

Spiritual Influence

Onyx helps you centre yourself and confers self-control. It also aids intuitive guidance and gives you the confidence and power to make decisions.

As a protective crystal, Onyx helps you detach from your emotions and repels negativity. It is useful to wear when dealing with the death of a loved one, as it assists the grieving process.

Onyx relieves stress and balances male and female energies in the body. It also promotes happiness and makes you feel inspired.

Physical Influence

Onyx strengthens bone marrow and is suitable for the feet. It is also helpful in quelling excess sexual energy, appetites, and other physical desires.

Opal

Colour
Variegated Opalescence, brick to hyacinth-red, milk-white, yellow, brown, or brownish yellow

Spiritual Influence

Opal is an absorptive crystal highly receptive to surrounding energies. It is ideal for divination and psychic work because it helps you attune to others. Place an Opal over your third eye to clear your mind and stimulate psychic perceptions and visions.

Opals are transparent and illustrious when surrounded by positive energy, but they become clouded and dull when they come into contact with negativity. For this reason, it is essential to cleanse Opals regularly to enhance their effectiveness.

Opals promote joy, creativity, and emotional balance. Because they contain a broad spectrum of colours, they can also be used to clear the Chakras.

Physical Influence

Opals have an invigorating effect on the body. They stimulate the pineal and pituitary glands.

Opals also improve eyesight and can assist in the treatment of boils.

Pearl (Oyster Shell)

Colour
Pearl - Off white

Spiritual Influence

Like a mother, a Pearl brings a sense of peace and harmony. It hates discord and will avoid it at every turn. Pearl gives a beginning when there is none and an ending when it needs to be done. It is also protective and sensitive to your needs.

When worn, it brings peace and tranquillity.

Physical Influence

Pearls look after all the main organs we cannot function without. I suggest you do not wear pearls if you don't want to conceive.

Peridot

Colour
Lime or olive green

Spiritual Influence

Peridot stimulates the mind and enhances intuition. It also aligns the Chakras and subtle bodies, allowing you to experience greater sensitivity, a higher level of awareness, and a deeper insight into your true-life path and purpose.

Peridot is often called "the crystal of personal growth." It helps you rise above envy, jealousy, insecurity, and the mundane concerns of everyday life. It promotes acceptance, broadens your philosophical perspective, and gives you the focus and dedication required to pursue your aspirations and desires.

Peridot also reduces stress, calms emotional turmoil, and opens new doors of experience. If you wear or carry it regularly, it will bring many new opportunities for you.

Physical Influence

Peridot balances the glandular system and enhances the health of the blood, heart, liver, spleen, and pancreas. It is also beneficial for those with hearing loss.

Because Peridot is an uplifting crystal, it is helpful for depression. It also promotes renewal and regeneration and assists in the healing of burns, cuts, and grazes.

Petrified Wood (Fossil)

Colour
Brown, reddish-brown, earth tone colours

Spiritual Influence

Petrified Wood is fossilised wood from trees. It has a calming, grounding vibration and eliminates stress and worries.

Petrified Wood is often placed in the home to repel negativity and protect against dark forces. Because it is millions of years old, it has been used in past life regression.

If you are experiencing upheaval, Petrified Wood can help you find your feet. It promotes peace and happiness and enables you to appreciate the simple things in life.

Physical Influence

Petrified Wood imbues its wearer with energy. It is also a powerful healer, beneficial for those with arterial sclerosis, arthritis, rheumatism, senility, and blood clots.

When worn frequently, Petrified Wood promotes thick, lustrous hair and strengthens the skin, muscles, and circulatory system.

Pyrite (Fool's Gold)

Colour
Gold-yellow

Spiritual Influence

Pyrite gives a sense of confidence and strength within. It gives courage and encouragement to do the impossible. Pyrite is a protective crystal for dangerous occupations or when driving long distances. It will help you forget bad memories and be surrounded by beautiful past experiences.

Physical Influence

Pyrite is an excellent tool for healing, circulation, and digestion. It is great for treating gout and preventing epidemics, so that you will be protected.

Rhodochrosite

Colour

Pink, reddish-brown with white streaks

Spiritual Influence

Rhodochrosite is a powerful transmitter of energy worn to attract love. It stimulates loving thoughts, feelings, and words in its wearer, as well as courage, motivation, and self-confidence, because it blends the driving energies of the base, sacral, and solar plexus Chakras with the loving energy of the heart Chakra.

A powerful emotional balancer, Rhodochrosite can aid in healing heartache and emotional wounds. It inspires acceptance, peace and self-love and enhances the intellect.

Physical Influence

Rhodochrosite is a healing crystal that helps regulate the heart, spleen, pituitary gland and blood circulation.

Rhodonite

Colour
Pink, red, reddish-brown,
sometimes with black streaks

Spiritual Influence

Rhodonite is a calming crystal that dispels anxiety and confusion. It also enhances mental and physical energy and balances the male and female polarities in the body.

Rhodonite is a helpful crystal to wear if you are feeling anxious or doubtful. It confers coherence, balance, and surety of purpose. It removes energy blockages and aligns the base and heart Chakras, which helps put love into action.

A crystal of deep feeling, Rhodonite enables you to understand that there is strength in being vulnerable.

Physical Influence

Rhodonite aids the immune and central nervous systems. It also helps to heal and strengthen the lungs, heart, joints, throat, and pancreas. Rhodonite is beneficial for those suffering from emphysema or arthritis.

Rose Quartz

Colour

Dark to pale pink

Spiritual Influence

Rose Quartz opens the heart Chakra, enabling you to give and receive love. It helps you realise that to accept love from another person, you must love yourself first.

If you have experienced emotional trauma, wear a Rose Quartz pendant, preferably over your heart. Rose quartz promotes healing, compassion, and forgiveness and encourages the release of suppressed emotions.

Rose Quartz also eases stress and tension and boosts self-esteem. It makes you respond to people and situations with compassion and sensitivity rather than logic. It helps you create and keep friends.

Physical Influence

Rose Quartz is a purifying crystal that releases toxins in the body and keeps the skin clear and radiant. It has a soothing effect on the heart, is beneficial for the kidneys and circulatory system, and aids respiratory stress due to bronchial infections.

Ruby

Colour

Red being the most prominent

Spiritual Influence

Ruby confers courage and inner strength and amplifies life force. It also helps to banish mental limitations, so it is a good crystal to wear when you need to drop any worries you have burdened yourself with to experience pleasure and joy.

A crystal of protection, a Ruby guards against negativity and danger. You will no longer fear your enemies if you wear or carry a Ruby. It makes you feel invincible, alert, and physically aware.

Rubies have long been valued as luck-attracting crystals, especially when worn on the left side of the body. They are believed to manifest wealth and love.

This crystal aids the wearer in finding courage when there is none to be found.

Physical Influence

A Ruby promotes vitality by stimulating the flow of energy throughout the body. It is especially beneficial for the heart and blood circulation.

Ruby's strengthening influence also enhances the immune system. It helps detoxify the blood and regenerate the body's tissues.

Rutilated Quartz

Colour

Smoky clear with Gold streaks

Spiritual Influence

When carried or worn, Rutilated Quartz dispels depression and raises energy. It helps you receive clear information from your higher self; regarding positive direction, creative inspiration, and self-realisation.

Rutilated Quartz emits more intense electric energy than Clear Quartz. It is a powerful tool for astral travel, past-life regression, and communicating with the spirit world. Rutilated Quartz is also helpful for divination because it increases clairvoyance.

Physical Influence

Rutilated Quartz aids tissue regeneration and strengthens the immune system. It is an excellent crystal to wear if you are ill, as it lends energy to the body and speeds the healing process.

This crystal is excellent for overall health.

Sapphire

Colour

Most colours of the rainbow – Blue is the most prominent

Spiritual Influence

Sapphire has a cool, healing vibration. Its deep blue reflects its ability to negate animosity and soothe frayed emotions.

When worn or carried, Sapphire confers a convivial, pleasant nature and encourages harmonious interactions. It protects against envy and negative energy and brings peace and happiness.

Sapphire is a valuable tool for meditation and divination because it promotes mental clarity. It balances and stimulates psychic awareness.

Sapphire also enhances creative inspiration and expression. It helps create a healthy connection between your body, mind, and spirit.

Physical Influence

Sapphire is used to relieve fevers and eye ailments. It is also carried as an amulet to protect general health, boost immunity, and strengthen the body's organs.

Selenite

Colour

Shimmering white or soft peach

Spiritual Influence

Selenite is purity in the making. This crystal's vibration is higher and more consistent with its mathematical pursuits. Selenite is excellent for meditations with deities, from God to Buddha. There is nothing this crystal can't connect with. Hold or wear a Selenite crystal when the head is fuzzy; you will find that clarity again.

If placed where it can be seen, Selenite protects those you love and your home from danger, creating a positive atmosphere of love and understanding. It can also unblock writing or an artist's creativity.

Physical Influence

Because of its calcium properties, it is a good crystal for teeth and bones.

Serpentine

Colour
Green (New Jade Red, green,
brown-yellow, and white)

Spiritual Influence

Serpentine is a mysterious crystal with many uses. It is protective, informative, and emotionally stable. Because of its Magnetite (Loadstone) influence, it is excellent for bringing money and wealth into your home.

Physical Influence

Serpentine can be worn to help with sexual dysfunctions, allowing individuals to focus on pleasure rather than the anxiety of it all. It also supports kidney health and can alleviate stomach pain related to gallbladder removal. It is also excellent for young girls starting their first menstrual cycle, as it can help relieve cramps.

Smoky Quartz

Colour
Translucent light smoky grey/brown

Spiritual Influence

Smoky Quartz is a protective, grounding crystal that balances masculine and feminine energy in the body and improves energy flow.

Carrying or wearing Smoky Quartz is useful when you need to let go of ideas and relationships that no longer support you. It can help you come to terms with the truth of a given situation and assist you in moving beyond the limitations of the conscious mind.

Smoky Quartz is also an uplifting crystal. It dispels depression and negativity and enhances the clarity of your dreams.

Physical Influence

Smoky Quartz has a mildly sedating effect on the body. It enhances the health of the kidneys, pancreas, and adrenal glands. It also helps you connect with your sexual energy in a healthy, balanced way.

Sodalite

Colour

Blue with white vein-like streaks

Spiritual Influence

Sodalite stabilises the mind and emotions and balances male and female energy in the body. It alleviates fear, calms inner conflict, and helps you recognise and verbalise your thoughts and feelings.

If you are feeling confused, meditate while holding a piece of Sodalite; it will calm the activity of your conscious mind and help you become clear about the issue that is bothering you.

Sodalite also confers insight, rationality, and good judgment. It is particularly beneficial for supersensitive individuals who are governed by their emotions.

Physical Influence

Sodalite is a soothing, healing crystal that relaxes the body. It helps to clear energy blockages in the thyroid gland and aids hormonal balance. It can also assist in the treatment of digestive disorders.

Sugilite

Colour

Purple with bands of black or indigo

Spiritual Influence

Sugilite attunes the mind to psychic insight and communication with the spirit world. It is utilised during meditation to open the third eye and awaken inner wisdom.

When worn or carried, Sugilite dissipates disturbing emotions such as stress, anger, fear, and depression. It can help to transform old negative thoughts and behaviour patterns into positive energy and advancement.

Sugilite lifts your vibration and imbues you with hope, confidence, and inspiration. It also promotes spiritual love.

Physical Influence

Sugilite is a healing crystal that enhances organ function and strengthens the endocrine system, particularly the pineal and pituitary glands.

Sunstone

Colour
Light Orange Pink

Spiritual Influence

Sunstone brings courage to new, uncertain situations. When carried, it is beneficial for children who are being bullied at school. Because of its colour, it enhances communication with spirit and psychic work. Sunstone is protective and expresses how we feel about those we love.

Sunstone facilitates sexual communication between partners.

Physical Influence

Sunstone speeds up healing from brain/head accidents, and aids with pain from arthritis, rheumatism, osteoporosis fractures, and other bone-related chronic pain.

Tiger Eye

Colour

Yellow, blue, and brown with a silky lustre & Hematite bands

Spiritual Influence

Tiger Eye is a strengthening crystal that empowers its wearer with courage and confidence. It encourages you to trust your intuitive impressions and confers an optimistic approach to life.

A "good luck" crystal, Tiger Eye, is believed to draw wealth and is often used in rituals to attract money. When given, it promotes fidelity and integrity, enhancing the bond that has grown between lovers.

Tiger Eye, when worn or carried, calms emotional turmoil and enhances objectivity. It can help you gain a clear perspective on the direction you should pursue when your life structure is changing.

Tiger Eye is excellent for children, as it wards off the evil eye and any negative vibration.

Physical Influence

Tiger Eye is ideal for those who are weak from illness, as it stimulates the flow of life force throughout the body. It also improves night vision and aids female problems associated with the naval Chakra.

When used in conjunction with Red Jasper and Carnelian Agate. A Tiger Eye is believed to assist conception.

Tiger Iron

Colour

Burnt red and brown with yellow streaks

Spiritual Influence

A blend of Hematite, Red Jasper, and Tiger Eye, Tiger Iron grounding and stabilising attunes you to the earth. It increases the strength of willpower and makes you passionate about your goals. It is an excellent crystal to wear when you need to "get the job done" without the encumbrance of doubt or hesitation.

Tiger's Iron is another protective crystal. When worn, it is believed to help its wearer find peace and refuge when danger is at hand.

Physical Influence

When held or worn, Tiger Iron transmits strong energy currents into the body. It promotes physical vitality and strength, and particularly benefits steroid production and muscular development.

Tiger's iron also enhances the assimilation of vitamin B.

Topaz

Colour
Blue, brown, greenish-brown,
yellow, red, or violet

Spiritual Influence

Topaz has an uplifting vibration, which is beneficial on many levels. It bestows courage and protection and drives away fear, anger, depression, and tension. It is a powerful tool for divination and meditation, as it expands psychic awareness and knowledge of the inner self. It is also a useful crystal for writers and scientists because it stimulates the intellect.

When carried or worn, Topaz is believed to draw love and abundance. When placed under your pillow during sleep, it promotes tranquillity and beautiful dreams.

Topaz is a soothing crystal that confers emotional balance. It is beneficial for those prone to addiction, as it assists in the control of undesirable habits.

Topaz highlights your individuality and can give you clear insight into your innate talents. It also enhances your charm and creative expression.

Physical Influence

Topaz helps regulate metabolism, digestion, and the nervous system. It enhances the health of the lungs and is believed to protect against colds and flu.

Topaz is also beneficial for the liver, aiding detoxification. It gives the skin a healthy, radiant glow and promotes tissue regeneration.

Tourmalinated Quartz

Colour
Black, brown, brownish-green, or pink

Spiritual Influence

Tourmalinated Quartz is a blend of Clear Quartz and Black Tourmaline, perfect for balancing male and female energy in the body. Black Tourmaline has an intense, protective energy that neutralises negativity, while Clear Quartz enhances psychism, clarity, and sensitivity.

A grounding crystal, Tourmalinated Quartz calms and relaxes the mind and promotes emotional balance. It is often utilised for meditation, as it assists concentration and clarity.

Tourmalinated Quartz dispels disturbing emotions such as anger, jealousy, fear, and depression. It is used in protection spells to shield against those who work with dark forces.

It also helps to align the Chakras and facilitate astral projection.

Physical Influence

Tourmalinated Quartz helps balance the endocrine system. It also has a revitalising effect on the body and mind.

Turquoise

Colour

Blue- Green

Spiritual Influence

Turquoise has been used for decades as a protection and wealth amulet. It helps to get your point across through persuasive, articulate communication and kindles passion and sincerity.

There is nothing we can't do or express when worn around the neck. It brings peace to turbulent circumstances and situations. It keeps friends loyal and close. It brings peace of mind to those who have just lost a loved one, as Amethyst does. The tranquillity this crystal engenders is genuine and trustworthy.

A must-have in any crystal pouch.

Physical Influence

Because of its healing and calming colour and properties, Turquoise can give respite from chronic conditions, alleviating pain and discomfort. It aids with muscle spasms and neurological complications. Turquoise is the healthy crystal, the one to keep us free of pain and grow old gracefully.

Unakite

Colour

Matt green with orange to pink patches

Spiritual Influence

Unakite is a grounding crystal with a balancing and healing effect on the emotions and heart Chakra.

Healers often use Unakite to assist in rebirthing, as it helps release the underlying emotional issues associated with an illness or problem.

When worn or carried, Unakite encourages you to examine your attitudes and feelings toward relationships and let go of the self-defeating belief that you are unworthy of love.

Unakite promotes a deep sense of inner peace and allows you to give and receive love freely without fear of being hurt.

Physical Influence

Unakite helps to regulate and heal the reproductive system. It is beneficial for pregnant women, as it aids the growth of the foetus.

Unakite balances sexual energy. It also aids those with eating disorders.

Zeolite

Colour

White and Green

Spiritual Influence

Zeolite projects a spiritual healing energy that understands what it takes to endure stressful and difficult situations. Because of its generic and combined minerals, it acts as a know-it-all and is used by people who want to learn more about spiritual awareness and their personal journey. Call it an all-purpose purse cleaner; it is good for just about everything.

Physical Influence

If you have an illness I have not discussed, please use Zeolite in all health .related issues due to its understanding of the physical body.

Zircon

Colour
Red, green, yellow or grey

Spiritual Influence

Zircon is a purifying crystal that balances the emotions and strengthens the mind. It also bestows self-esteem.

When worn, Zircon can help you let go of deeply ingrained beliefs that perpetuate a lack of self-worth and inhibit your potential. It dispels depression, raises energy, and encourages you to fulfil your goals and dreams.

Physical Influence

Zircon helps to regulate the pituitary and pineal glands. It can also assist in the treatment of bowel problems and insomnia.

Metals

Copper

Colour

Brownish Orange

Spiritual Influence

Copper sorts out your thoughts and amplifies the energy field when worn or carried. It is helpful for intensive study, particularly if you are researching a difficult subject.

Copper is a powerful magical tool because it is an effective conductor of energy. In spells and rituals, copper magnifies magical intent.

Copper also builds self-esteem and confidence and can help restore your faith in life.

Physical Influence

Copper balances the body's energy flow, aids healing, and protects against illness. Bracelets made from copper have long been worn to help relieve the symptoms of arthritis, rheumatism, and bursitis.

Copper also enhances blood circulation and helps fight bacteria and infection.

Gold

Colour
Gold

Spiritual Influence

Gold is a power-enhancing metal that can help you attune to the sun's energy. It purifies and energises the body spiritually, mentally, and physically. It also balances the energy of the right and left brain and promotes positive thinking.

Gold enhances courage and confidence and is believed to protect against danger when worn or carried. It is also used in rituals to attract money, success, and wisdom.

Physical Influence

Wearing Gold as jewellery is believed to bestow strength and enhance health, promoting longevity. Gold is particularly beneficial for the nervous system and is helpful in addressing digestive and circulatory issues.

Meteorite

Colour

Black, Grey with Gold Tones

Spiritual and Physical Influence

Meteorites are small pieces of solid mineral matter from outer space. They are the product of what we have termed "shooting stars". As Meteorites enter the Earth's atmosphere, they heat up, causing brilliant light flashes as they fall to the ground.

Meteorite facilitates thought transmission and telepathic communication. It expands your awareness and helps you connect with extraterrestrial energies.

A purifying crystal, Meteorite is worn to strengthen the energy field and balance masculine and feminine energy in the body. It is also an excellent meditation tool. Hold a piece of Meteorite above your third eye to enhance your vision.

Silver

Colour

Silver

Spiritual Influence

Silver enhances psychic receptivity and awareness and promotes emotional balance and creativity. It is associated with the goddess Diana. It is used in rituals and divination to invoke her presence.

If you ever find yourself so wrapped up in fear or nervousness that you begin to stifle your intuition and lose your objectivity, wearing Silver will calm your thoughts and help you face a situation with clarity and confidence.

You can wear Silver to attract love and money and show courage when taking emotional chances. It encourages you to listen to your inner self while walking the path of destiny.

Physical Influence

Although Silver predominantly influences emotions and the psychic mind, it has a cleansing and healing effect on the body and aids detoxification and circulation.

When worn below the waist, Silver enhances fertility and relieves stress.

Crystal Zodiac Signs

Astrology is a widely popular method for predicting future events. You can turn the pages of a newspaper and see what your daily Zodiac holds for you. You can turn the dial on your car radio and hear relationship and financial advice influenced by your Zodiac Sign, your Sun sign. There are Zodiac Sign Apps for smartphones; you can even email an Astrologist for a more thorough interpretation. Some people would not make a move unless they consulted an astrologist for financial or relationship issues, as our ancestors did for planting and seeding by charting the stars so long ago.

How often have you heard a work colleague say, "My Zodiac Sign says it is a good day for love or a change"? We have all tapped into astrology at some point. Seventy per cent of the world's population know their Sun sign. It is often assumed that you know it when asked, and if you don't, don't worry; they will help you find it by asking for your date of birth. However, astrology is more complex than what you read in the media, and the authenticity may not be entirely accurate.

People will tell you that some of the daily predictions are way off the mark, and I can certainly vouch for that, but others are spot on. It depends on who is doing it and how genuine they are, not just a computer-generated report with generic information. Some astrologists use computer charts, which perform calculations as they are fed all your personal information, including the exact time and place of your birth. The Earth's rotation at any given time differs by continent.

Crystals are a big part of your star sign and offer valuable insights into the physical, mental, emotional, and spiritual factors that influence our personalities. Each crystal's strength corresponds to a Zodiac sign to enhance or mitigate character traits or flaws.

Aries (21 March – 19 April)
Fire Sign
Crystals: Traditional and Alternative - Garnet and Rose Quartz

Arians are forthright, impulsive, action-oriented people who sometimes struggle to slow down and listen to their inner selves. They are prone to headaches and stress. Arians need to learn to consider the long-term consequences of their actions and be more tolerant of people who move slower than they do. They are happiest when they have an outlet for their abundant energy and drive, a specific goal they can see to completion.

Taurus (20 April – 20 May)
Earth Sign
Crystals: Traditional and Alternative - Emerald and Chrysoprase

Taureans are reliable, steadfast people who value security in relationships and careers. Although they are generally easy-going and placid, they can be stubborn and suffer from blocked emotions and expression; spontaneity and flexibility do not come easily to them. Taureans need to learn to let go and move with the ebb and flow of life. They are happiest when their intense need for love, sensuality, and beauty is fulfilled.

Gemini (21 May – 20 June)
Air Sign
Crystals: Traditional and Alternative - Pearl and Moonstone

Geminis are quick, chatty, versatile people who do not like to be tied down to any one place or person. They thrive on mental stimulation, excitement, and change and love exploring new horizons. However, their aspirations would be better realised if they were more grounded and spent more time straightening out the day-to-day details of their lives. Geminis are at their best when they can put their diverse talents into practice.

Cancer (21 June – 22 July)
Water Sign
Crystals: Traditional and Alternative - Ruby and Carnelian Agate

Cancerians are sensitive, moody, and extremely self-protective. They value a comfortable and secure domestic environment where they can retreat when feeling super sensitive. Emotional disturbances affect Cancerians deeply and can manifest in stomach upsets. When it comes to love relationships, Cancerians tend to base their world around their partner and are extremely clingy. They need to learn to overcome their insecurities and develop more independence. Cancerians are warm, nurturing, and compassionate towards others.

Leo (23 July – 22 August)
Fire Sign
Crystals: Traditional and Alternative- Peridot and Spinel

Leos are confident, courageous, and ambitious. They are often very dramatic and love to be the centre of attention. If they do not feel appreciated or have the freedom to exercise their brilliant capabilities, they can become bitter and frustrated and take it out on those around them. When their creativity is not allowed free rein, they are prone to emotional blockages and poor circulation. Leos need to use their ingenuity to thoroughly evaluate themselves so that they can better understand their goals and motivations. Mostly, they are warm, loving, open-hearted, and fun to be around.

Virgo (23 August – 22 September)
Earth Sign
Crystals: Traditional and Alternative
-Sapphire (Blue)

Virgos are responsible, methodical, highly-strung people with a practical life approach. They tend to be critical and pedantic and can offend others without realising it. They need to learn to relax and look at the bigger picture of life, so they don't become bogged down by the petty details. Virgos tend to worry and hold on to negative programming; this can lead to digestive problems such as constipation, diarrhoea, and irritable bowel syndrome. Virgos are happiest in a peaceful, balanced environment where their needs are understood and respected.

Libra (23 September – 22 October)
Air Sign
Crystals: Traditional and Alternative
-Sapphire (Blue)

Librans are charming, diplomatic people who value balance and harmony. Although they like to avoid conflict, sometimes they inadvertently create it due to their inconsistent approach to other people—Librans tend to swing from one extreme to the other before they rest in the centre. It is impossible to fool a Libran; they are very perceptive and great strategists. They value partnerships based on love and understanding and admire style, beauty, and elegance.

Scorpio (23 October – 21 November)
Water Sign
Crystals: Traditional and Alternative Topaz and Citrine

Scorpios are magnetic and intense yet highly private and secretive. They experience the world through their feelings and emotions and do not like giving too much away until they feel they can trust someone. Revenge and retaliation are second nature to them if they feel betrayed. Scorpios need to come to terms with their suspicion and insecurity, and their tendency to be ruled by sexual desire. They have the strength and endurance to let go of behaviour patterns that sabotage themselves and others.

Sagittarius (22 November – 21 December)
Fire Sign
Crystals: Traditional and Alternative - Tanzanite and Blue Topaz

Sagittarians are gregarious, fun, and often very playful. They have a philosophical and hedonistic approach to life, but are usually hard to tie down as they crave new experiences. Sagittarians have an insatiable desire for adventure and conquest and tend to overlook the practical details of their grand plans and schemes. They do not appreciate moderate advice from others, as they see it as an attempt to squash their enthusiasm. Although they can be unreliable, Sagittarians are very lovable. People are drawn to them for their warmth, honesty, and charisma.

Capricorn (22 December – 19 January)
Earth Sign
Crystals: Traditional and Alternative - Garnet and Rose Quartz

Capricorns are serious, thoughtful, and profound. They believe success equals hard work, as they do not expect opportunities to fall in their laps. Capricorns can appear calm and somewhat out of reach, but this is simply a mask they wear to protect themselves from being hurt or rejected. Although they may not show it, they are sensitive and become very depressed when others let them down. Capricorns are reliable, consistent, and trusting but rigid and inflexible. They need to let go of negative thoughts and behaviour patterns and learn to lighten up and appreciate the joy of life.

Aquarius (20 January – 19 February)
Air Sign
Crystals: Traditional and Alternative - Amethyst and Amber

Aquarians are open-minded and accepting of others, but extremely fixed in their lifestyle, belief structure, and behaviour patterns. They are fiercely individualistic and can always offer a unique perspective on any issue. They laugh in the face of authority, approaching problems logically and unemotionally. Aquarians need to get in touch with emotions and feelings—their own and other people's. They are prone to stress, tension and anxiety due to mental overactivity and emotional imbalance.

Pisces (20 February – 20 March)
Water Sign
Crystals: Traditional and Alternative - Aquamarine and Jade

Pisceans are sensitive, compassionate, and highly creative. They become unhappy and disgruntled without an outlet for their unique talents and complex inner world. They are easily disillusioned and prone to addictions. Pisceans are highly susceptible to the energies around them, so they need a calm and tranquil home environment. They need to learn the art of detachment so that when subjected to uncomfortable emotions such as tension, stress, and anger, they do not take on the mood of their environment.

Crystals and The Chakras

The human body is as much an energetic entity as it is a material form. Seven spinning wheels of energy known as "Chakras" line the spine from the tailbone to the crown of the head. Each reflects a specific set of mental, emotional, physical, and spiritual characteristics, characterised by different colours and frequencies.

Thoughts, emotions, and the energies of the surrounding environment affect the health and well-being of the Chakras.

The Chakras are spiritual Lotus flowers. Each one has its own emotional and spiritual function. The Kundalini, our energy force, is depicted as a snake that travels up and down the Chakra ladder, from the Muladhara, the Root Chakra, to the Anahata, the Heart Chakra. This action keeps our energy force activated and at harmonious levels. However, due to spiritual or emotional upsets caused by an individual or situation, the Kundalini may lodge itself in one particular Chakra and become stagnant, unable to energise the rest of the Chakras.

If you're feeling depressed, it could be impacting your Root Chakra, which is located at the base of your spine. It's essential to address the issues causing this depression; otherwise, your Kundalini energy may become stagnant, hindering the activation of your life force. This stagnation can create a chain reaction that affects your Navel Chakra and Solar Plexus, leading to overwhelming feelings that permeate every aspect of your being, even reaching your Crown Chakra.

Depression often results in a lack of energy, decreased enthusiasm, and a pervasive sense of unworthiness or loneliness. These feelings might be linked to blockages in your Chakras due to emotional distress. By investigating and confronting the root causes of your depression, you can start to work through these emotions, allowing your Kundalini energy to flow freely again. Once the energy is unblocked, it can revitalise your life force across all Chakras, promoting healing and renewal.

Crystals are powerful tools for strengthening and fortifying the chakras. Chakras emit and absorb specific types of electromagnetic energy, helping to restore balance and vitality to your entire life force.

Music plays a vital role in our lives. When we listen to a piece of music, we may either enjoy it immediately or dislike it. We sometimes find ourselves playing a particular song on repeat, yet at a certain point, we suddenly stop and move on to something else. This shift occurs because one of the seven chakras is blocked and resonates with the musical frequency and the particular note it was played or sung to. Once that Chakra stabilises, the kundalini can continue its journey, leaving us feeling peaceful and rejuvenated, all because of a single musical note.

Next time you play a song more than four times in a day, you know there is a Chakra that needs the frequency.

I have added songs to each Chakra and the note the artist played and sang it on.

There are many crystals for each Chakra, and a fun way to experiment until you find the right one. Crystal colour is of great importance in Chakra healing and balancing. The Chakras are vibrant and fluctuate in intensity depending on our moods. The objective is to maintain the Chakra balance; you don't want the Lotus flower open; if it is, that Chakra is excessive, and if it's closed, it is deficient, so the goal is to keep it just in the middle where it is its happiest. Our emotional well-being will benefit from it.

When performing a Chakra cleansing, hold the appropriate crystal over the Chakra you wish to treat and visualise its colour becoming more transparent and translucent. Breathe deeply to clear the mind and energise the body. Concentrate on channelling positive, nurturing thoughts to encourage a free energy flow. Clearing blockages and imbalances from the Chakras has a fantastic effect on how you think and feel.

Muladhara - The Root Chakra
Colour   Red
Crystal   Red Jasper
Musical Note   C (Do)

Songs: *"Let It Be" by the Beatles, "Clocks" by Coldplay, "Ode to Joy" by Beethoven, "Canon" by Pachelbel,*

"Fugue in E Minor" by Beethoven, "Stand By Me" by Ben E. King, and "You Raise Me Up" by Josh Groban.

The root Chakra is located at the base of the spine and is associated with physical and sexual energy and the fight/flight response. Its energy kicks into action when you are in danger or under attack. Feelings such as anger, courage, and sexual desire trigger it. The root Chakra grounds the rest of the Chakra system.

Your root Chakra is balanced and healthy if you feel alert and strong with the drive to handle your challenges. However, if the energy of your root Chakra is stifled, it can lead to feelings of powerlessness and limitation.

To keep the Root Chakra balanced, use a Red Jasper crystal. Use a Blue Lace Agate crystal to calm the excessive Chakra and keep emotions like anger, aggression towards yourself and others, and any other destructive energy out of your Chakra. If your root Chakra is deficient, you could feel unsafe, unwanted, weak, or unloved. Treat your deficient root Chakra with a Ruby crystal.

Svadhisthana - The Abdominal (navel) Chakra

Colour Orange
Crystal Tiger Eye
Musical Note D (Re)

Songs: *"She Will Be Loved"* by Maroon 5, *"Knocking On Heaven's Door"* by Eric Clapton, *"Just the Way You Are"* by Bruno Mars, *Symphony no. 2 in D Major"* by Beethoven, and *"Free Fallin' "* by Tom Petty.

The sacral Chakra is located between the navel and the pubic bone. It reflects your sexual identity, unique balance of masculine and feminine energy, and emotional needs and behaviours. This Chakra is highly responsive to the thoughts and feelings of others and to the energy of your surrounding environment.

When the sacral Chakra is balanced, you can connect with your emotions and relate to others in a healthy and balanced way. In this state, a Tiger Eye crystal can help keep you grounded. However, your Chakra may be excessive if you feel overwhelmed by others' emotions or are caught up in your own dramatic episodes. In such cases, a Lapis Lazuli can help bring it under control. Conversely, if you feel dull and lifeless, out of touch with your emotions, and lacking in sexual intimacy, your sacral Chakra may be deficient. Carrying a Carnelian crystal can help elevate your masculine or feminine energy levels to restore balance.

Manipura - The Solar Plexus Chakra

Colour Yellow
Crystal Citrine
Musical Note E (Mi)

Songs: "*Sweet Home Alabama*" by Lynyrd Skynyrd, "*Every Breath You Take*" by The Police, "*Violin Concerto in E Major*" by Bach, "*Born to Run*" by Bruce Springsteen, "*Don't Stop Believin'* " by Journey and "*More Than Words*" by Extreme.

The solar plexus Chakra is located between the navel and lower ribs and is associated with intuitive awareness, or your "gut feeling," your personal power, and your sense of self. It acts as the Chakra system's gatekeeper, alerting you to potentially threatening situations and encouraging you to put your own needs first. Citrine will help you make this happen.

When your solar plexus Chakra is balanced, you feel confident, self-assured, and in control of your life. But when unbalanced, you may compromise your power and allow other people to manipulate you. This can lead to persistent fits of anger and resentment or depression and despair. You may also experience an unaccustomed drain on your energy.

If the Solar Plexus becomes excessive, you want to be the centre of attention, think you are more intelligent than everyone, and do not listen to what you are saying. An Amethyst crystal helps tone this excessive Chakra; if it's deficient, you could feel depressed and confused and ignore your gut feeling. You may also think that you are being controlled by others or bullied to the point of not wanting to be alone. For this, you must work with an

Amber crystal to strengthen the Solar Plexus and function emotionally without being intimidated.

Anahata - The Heart Chakra
Colour   **Green**
Crystal   **Aventurine**
Musical Note F (Fa)

Songs: *"All of Me" by John Legend, "If I Ain't Got You" by Alicia Keys, "The Climb" by Miley Cyrus, "I Will Always Love You" by Whitney Houston, "Clair de Lune" by Debussy, "Minuet in F" by Mozart, and "We Are the Champions" by Queen.*

The heart Chakra is in the centre of the chest behind the sternum and reflects how you give and receive love. It is also the vital link for communication between the Chakras below it and the Chakras above.

When your heart Chakra is healthy and balanced, you can give and receive love freely and spontaneously without being dependent on the love of others. It endows you with self-love and the ability to love; the Aventurine crystal will aid you in maintaining the above.

However, if your heart Chakra is too open compared to the other Chakras, you will tend to direct most of its energy outwards, leaving little for yourself, and you will need to work with a Rose Quartz crystal. If your heart Chakra is closed, you may be reluctant to give or ask for love for fear of being hurt. Over time, this can lead you to become cold, apathetic, isolated, divided between the physical and the spiritual, and scared to let go. You can work with a Bloodstone crystal to restore it to its healthy state again.

Vishuddha - The Throat Chakra
Colour   Blue
Crystal   Sodalite
Musical Note G (Sol)

Songs: *"Amazing Grace / The Entertainer" by Scott Joplin, "Let Her Go" by Passenger, "Gavotte in G Major" by Handel, Riptide by Vance Joy, and "Hallelujah" by Leonard Cohen.*

The throat Chakra is located in the centre of the throat and is associated with expression, release and transformation. It channels information from the body and spirit Chakras into tangible expression. It is associated with singing, writing, and public speaking.

In a balanced Chakra system, the throat Chakra endows you with the ability to verbalise your physical, spiritual, and emotional needs and express your feelings clearly. It also enables you to speak your truth appropriately.

However, suppose your throat Chakra is blocked, which can happen often. In that case, you may be afraid to express how you feel and become overburdened with stifled emotions you cannot release to the point of sore throats, laryngitis, tonsillitis, and even cancer. Typical symptoms of a blocked throat Chakra include tightly controlled behaviour, emotional tension and an unwillingness to change. Still, you can work with Aquamarine to combat all the above.

Suppose you experience an addictive personality and speak without thinking, not concerned about others' emotions, and not caring who hears it. In that case, you have a very aggressive, excessive chakra, which you need to address as soon as possible, and you can do that with Howlite.

Ajna - Third Eye Chakra
Colour   Indigo / Purple
Crystal   Amethyst
Musical Note   A (La)

Songs: *"Rolling in the Deep" by Adele, Sweet Child O' Mine" by Guns N' Roses, "Piano Sonata No.2 in A Major" by Beethoven, "Valerie" by Amy Winehouse.*

The third eye Chakra is located in the middle of the forehead, just above the eyebrows. It bestows intuition and discernment and helps you to see yourself and others objectively.

When the energy of your third eye Chakra is flowing freely, you can trust your clear perceptions and intuition and make wise decisions quickly with certainty. You can read people very easily and find it challenging to tolerate deception. Your insight may be so acute that you experience clairvoyance. To maintain this psychic connection, an Amethyst or a Lapiz Lazuli crystal is advisable.

When your third eye Chakra is excessive, it can infuse too much input, especially spiritual input, which can block your connection with the Universal forces. You can even get stuck in your reality and over-interpret the daily happenings. For this, using Yellow Calcite to bring you back down is best. If the Third eye is deficient, you can feel sluggish or reluctant to face the truth about yourself, your relationships, your true-life path, and your purpose. Common symptoms include confusion, absent-mindedness, vagueness, and lack of inspiration. For this, it is best to work with Azurite.

Sahasrara - The Crown Chakra
Colour   Pink
Crystal   Rose / Clear Quartz
Musical Note B (Ti)

Songs: *"Because Of You" by Kelly Clarkson, "Style" by Taylor Swift, "Man in the Mirror" by Michael Jackson, "You Are The Reason" by Calum Scott, "Piano Sonata No.3 in B-flat Major" by Mozart, and "Forever" by Chris Brown.*

The crown Chakra is located at the top of the head and is associated with the divine intelligence of the Universe and higher levels of awareness. It transmits information related to the spirit world, creative inspiration, self-realisation, and personal growth.

When your crown Chakra is active, and your entire Chakra system is balanced, you will be receptive to information and insights that encourage you to look beyond the surface of your existence and follow your creative instincts. The ideas you receive may come entirely out of left field, but they will be clear and meaningful, nonetheless. An excellent crystal for this is Rose Quartz.

Suppose you feel frustrated on an everyday basis to the point of depression or some manic episodes, like making decisions without thought or unexpected outbursts of fear and feelings. In that case, you could be suffering from excessive Chakra energy, which can activate a bipolar disorder if not addressed, and you can do that with Rose Quartz and Clear Quartz.

A deficient crown Chakra can manifest in no joy for life, being unable to accomplish everyday tasks, not listening because of your fear of the unknown, and not making decisions due to your insecurities. Other common symptoms include brain fog, poor memory, headaches, and insomnia. The quicker you address this, the better you will be. Use a Garnet crystal to lift your spirits and assure you that no matter what happens, Universal forces are on your side to guide you through it.

So, let's keep those Chakras in harmony with the help of crystals and music. Every morning in the shower, sing the Do Re Mi song from The Sound of Music. Each note activates each one of the Chakras. Make this song your mantra for cultivating harmony within yourself and your spirit.

Crystals For The Home

Our home is one of the most sacred places one could ever have. The thought of coming home after a long trip or relaxing after a hard day's work is priceless. We all want to go home to feel safe behind those protective walls when a storm approaches. Home is where our beloved pets are. Home is where we have our friends around for dinner or a barbecue. Home is where we cry, laugh, and sometimes fight with lovers, children, parents, friends, or neighbours, but no matter what, home is home.

Having a crystal as a centrepiece is a beautiful ornament, but having a crystal in the home for a purpose is smart. Crystals will protect your homes if you programme them to do so. They will combat illnesses, negativity, fights, arguments, or loss of income. They will always keep unwanted visitors or thieves away. They can bring financial security, love, or harmony to all the home residents, not to mention unlimited joy, laughter, and comfort.

Just by having crystals in your home, you know you are and will always be protected from unknown negativity that can creep in, such as others' negative thoughts and actions directed against you or a loved one. Think of crystals as your protection agency. We all need one of those now and then.

As I have said before, the size of a crystal is irrelevant; what matters is the connection you make with it.

Anything with a point directs energy to a specific location. A round crystal serves as a communication tool within the home, directing energy to facilitate comfortable interactions; this is why spheres are particularly effective for groups or family gatherings.

Crystals are used in many ways in the home, and here are a few examples. However, remember always to cleanse and programme your crystal for a particular intent, give it a mission or a task, and make it open to all things positive that can enter your home.

Agates come in many different shades of brown, orange, and grey. These beautiful crystals can inspire courage to stand up for yourself. They are excellent crystals for children bullied at school to have in their rooms. A brown agate can help someone who is quitting an addiction, like cigarettes or alcohol, if it is placed where that person usually sits in the home. Agate is one of those crystals you should always have at home due to its protective nature.

Amethyst is calming and soothing. It brings peaceful and calming energies to the home. It helps prevent arguments and discord, and if placed near someone with a temper, it can help calm them and encourage them to see reason. Amethyst will help alleviate stress in the home and reduce anxiety. An Amethyst in the home will aid communication during heated discussions. It is best placed where the family gets together.

Citrine can bring abundance to the home, such as love, happiness, and financial stability. It can also aid children in retaining lessons learned while studying and retaining information. Citrine fosters patience in uncomfortable situations and helps when dealing with teenagers. It can be placed in the living area of your home.

Clear Quartz protects your home and your loved ones from unwanted negative energies. Place a Clear Quartz rough point in the four corners of your home, with the points facing outward; this will help keep negativity at bay. Additionally, a sphere or a generator can be placed in a loved one's room if they have been ill. It will absorb whatever ailment they may have.

Rose Quartz is often considered the must-have crystal for the home. It brings love and understanding between a child and a parent, a husband and a wife, between lovers or partners. Rose Quartz communicates with our guides to help us love and understand the connection between the Universal forces. If a piece of Rose Quartz is placed in a family member's room who lacks self-love, it will help them feel better about themselves. It will help alleviate respiratory complications associated with the cold and flu season, especially if placed under the pillow.

A Crystal For Each Day Of The Week

Each planet in our solar system has unique attributes, colour, and crystal corresponding to the energy it brings. Utilising a specific crystal for a particular day of the week, corresponding to the planet of that week, can enhance your needs for that day. It's incredible how a little know-how can aid your everyday needs and the expectations you want to bring forth that day.

You can organise your crystals for the week if you wish; it doesn't hurt to be prepared if you know your schedule for that week. Ensure you have the corresponding planet and crystal required for the day's need. If you are going on a date on Friday, get a Rose Quartz ready and focus on the planet Venus. If you know you are going to a stressful situation at work, carry a Garnet to give you the strength needed while evoking the planet Mars to provide you with the confidence required to get through it.

The following is a list of the planet's attributes and the corresponding crystals for each day of the week.

Sun
Colour Yellow

Sunday is the healing day. Anything that needs to be mended physically or emotionally can be addressed on this day. Sunday is a good day of the week to work on home protection, plan new business transactions, or sell a home. The best crystal to use on Sundays is a Citrine.

When you wear or carry a Citrine, you will feel the Sun's energy and strength as it heals the mind, body, and spirit.

Moon
Colour White

Monday is excellent for working with your psychic abilities. Mondays are miraculous as they are complete with goodness in all aspects of human nature. You can work on your psychic ability, meditation or any spiritual endeavour you wish to achieve. Mondays are good for healing, understanding, peace and tranquillity, and you can use a Clear Quartz to reach for all you need or want.

Mars
Colour Red

Tuesday is the day of strength and fighting for your beliefs. It is a good day of the week to stand up to any individual or to make your point loud and clear at work or at home. Tuesday gives you the strength to fight for what you know is right and to have the support of others who feel the same way as you do. Tuesdays promote passion when Garnet is worn, and if you ever wanted to find that inner fighting strength, you could find it within on Tuesdays while meditating.

Mercury
Colour Burnt Orage-Brown

Wednesdays fall under communication. If you want to talk to someone about something that means a lot to you, this is the day to do it. Wednesday is a great day for couples to exchange views, conclude an ongoing altercation, and get their point across. Wednesdays give you wisdom and togetherness without stress when you wear an Amethyst.

Jupiter
Colour Blue

Thursday is the money day, a day when you work on any legal problem for a positive outcome. You can also work on personal goals and make them happen with the persistence of Thursdays. You will also be able to express your inner feelings without hurting those you love, while learning patience and achieving harmony within, with the help of a Sodalite crystal for the day.

Venus
Colour Pink

Friday is the day of love. This day enriches your passion or the love you desire and seek. Friday is the day for romantic get-togethers or getaways. Friday is an excellent day of the week to meet someone for the first time for a coffee or a drink. For a positive outcome, ensure you have a Rose Quartz crystal with you to enhance the loving energy around you.

Saturn
Colour Black

Saturday is a great day to clean your home and thoroughly clean out to make room for the new. Saturdays are an excellent day to get rid of negative individuals you no longer want around. Saturdays can rid you of your negativity if you carry an Onyx crystal to help you feel good about yourself and create a new positive outlook for the week ahead.

Closing

Every crystal contains a mystery that is exciting to unravel. Once you tap into a crystal's unique beauty and strength, the effect is transformational.

Crystals play a big part in my life. I cannot imagine my life without them. In troubled times, I have held or worn a Sodalite crystal to calm the storms in my heart. I have used Clear Quartz to strengthen and clarify my spiritual work. I used Amethyst while going through breast cancer, in conjunction with conventional medicine, to help manage my emotions and fortify my strength, allowing me to see a light at the end of the tunnel.

When worn or carried, crystals transmit a feeling of peace. A sense of spiritual enlightenment warms the heart like a candle amid darkness. Anger becomes a thing of the past. You exude love and compassion to those around you and learn to accept life's ups and downs.

Ileana

A Quick Reference Guide to Crystal Healing

A

Absorption	Charoite
Abuse - Verbal	Jade
Abundance	Citrine, Emerald
Acceptance	Charoite, Peridot, Rhodochrosite
Accident - Prevention	Carnelian, Chrysoprase
Aches	Lazurite
Acne	Obsidian, & Snowflake Obsidian
Acidity	Citrine, Peridot
Actors	Alexandrite, Bloodstone
Addiction	Alexandrite, Amethyst, Kunzite, Labradorite, Lepidolite, Topaz
Adrenal Glands	Smoky Quartz
Advancements	Charoite
Adversaries	Pyrite
Ageing	Rhodochrosite, Sodalite
Aggression	Bloodstone

Ailments	Lazurite, Sapphire
Alcoholism	Amethyst
Aliens	Copal
Allergies	Carnelian Agate, Zircon
Allure	Amber
Ambition	Howlite
Anaemia	Bloodstone, Citrine, Ruby
Angels	Celestine
Anger	Blue Lace Agate, Amethyst, Fluorite, Lapis Lazuli, Lepidolite, Sugilite, Topaz, Tourmalinated Quartz
Angina	Emerald
Animals	Aventurine
Animosity	Sapphire
Anxiety	Aventurine, Azurite, Lapis Lazuli, Lepidolite, Moonstone, Pyrite, Rhodonite, Serpentine
Anxious	Rhodonite
Arguments	Blue Lace Agate
Arterial Scoliosis	Petrified Wood
Arthritis	Amazonite, Copper, Malachite, Petrified Wood, Rhodonite, Sunstone
Articulate	Turquoise
Artist	Alexandrite, Selenite

Artistic Pursuits	Apatite
Aspiration	Peridot
Asthma	Amber, Rose Quartz, Azurite with Malachite, Malachite
Atral - Projection	Tourmalinated Quartz
Astral - Travel	Rutilated Quartz
Attraction	Amber, Moss Agate
Aura	Amethyst, Diamond, Garnet, Kunzite, Zircon
Auric Field	Jasper - Red
Awareness	Apophyllite, Celestine, Meteorite, Peridot

B

Babies	Rhodochrosite, Sodalite, Tiger Eye
Back pain	Carnelian, Celestine, Petrified Wood
Bad tempers	Amethyst, Blue Lace Agate, Rose Quartz
Bacteria	Copper
Beauty	Amber
Beginnings	Amethyst, Pearl
Behaviour	Carnelian Agate
Birth	Copal, Moonstone
Bites	Emerald

Bladder	Jade
Bleeding	Bloodstone, Ruby
Blockages	Clear Quartz
Blockages - Energy	Sodalite
Blood	Garnet, Hematite, Kunzite, Tiger Iron
Blood - Circulation	Copper, Ruby
Blood - Clots	Amethyst, Hematite, Petrified Wood
Blood - Pressure	Apatite
Body - Repair	Apatite
Boils	Opal, Sapphire
Bone Marrow	Onyx
Bones	Amazonite, Emerald, Fluorite, Howlite, Obsidian, & Snowflake, Rose Quartz, Selenite, Sunstone
Bowels	Obsidian, Yellow Jasper, Zircon
Brain	Amber, Azurite, Citrine, Fluorite, Gold
Brain waves	Labradorite
Breathing	Aventurine, Carnelian Agate
Broken heart	Amethyst, Rose Quartz
Bronchitis	Amber

Bruises	Rose Quartz
Bully	Sunstone
Burns	Chrysoprase, Peridot
Business	Citrine, Jet
Bursitis	Copper

C

Calcium	Amazonite, Calcite, Fluorite, Howlite, Selenite
Calm	Amethyst, Azurite, Celestine, Lazurite, Peridot, Sodalite Petrified Wood, Turquoise, Petrified Wood, Turquoise
Cancer	All Crystals, Amethyst, Emerald, Fluorite, Smoky Quartz, Alexandrite
Cardiovascular	Bloodstone
Cataracts	Charoite
Cervix	Copal
Chakras	All Crystals
Change	Charoite
Channelling	Calcite, Moldavite
Charm	Topaz
Chemotherapy	Malachite
Chest	Azurite

Childbirth	Bloodstone, Jasper - Red, Moonstone
Children	Tiger Eye
Chronic Health Conditions	Blue Quartz, Turquoise
Chronic Pain	Amethyst, Celestine, Sunstone, Turquoise
Circulatory - System	Agate, Azurite with Malachite, Gold, Moss Agate, Petrified Wood, Pyrite, Rose Quartz, Silver
Circumstances	Zeolite
Clairvoyance	Lapis Lazuli, Ruby, Rutilated Quartz
Clarity	Aquamarine, Fluorite, Jade, Lapis Lazuli, Lazurite, Silver Smoky Quartz, Tourmalinated Quartz
Coherence	Rhodonite
Colds	Carnelian Agate, Jet, Topaz
Colon	Tiger Eye, Yellow Jasper
Coma	Labradorite
Communication	Calcite, Clear Quartz, Chrysocolla, Howlite, Moldavite, Silver Sugilite, Sunstone, Turquoise
Compassion	Garnet, Azurite with Malachite, Chrysoprase, Emerald, Garnet, Moonstone, Rose Quartz
Composure	Moonstone

Concentration	Calcite, Carnelian, Citrine, Fluorite, Tourmalinated Quartz
Conception	Carnelian Agate, Red Jasper and Tiger Eye (all three together)
Conclusion	Lazurite
Confidence	Copper, Gold, Jasper -Red, Moonstone Obsidian & Snowflake Obsidian, Onyx, Pyrite, Rhodochrosite, Rose Quartz, Sugilite, Silver Tiger Eye
Confidence - Self	Rhodochrosite
Confusion	Apatite, Apophyllite, Azurite, Charoite, Rhodonite, Sodalite
Conjunctivitis	Apophyllite
Conscious	Sodalite
Consciousness	Diamond
Cough	Amber, Topaz
Courage	Aquamarine, Bloodstone, Dentritic Agate, Diamond, Garnet, Gold, Hematite, Jade, Labradorite, Lapis Lazuli, Pyrite, Silver, Sunstone, Topaz, Tiger Eye
Cramps	Bloodstone, Selenite, Serpentine

Creative Expression	Alexandrite, Bloodstone, Opal, Smoky Quartz, Rutilated Quartz, Topaz
Creativity	Celestine, Alexandrite, Apatite, Aventurine, Bloodstone, Celestine, Selenite, Silver
Crying	Coral
Cuts	Peridot

D

Dancers	Bloodstone
Danger	Apache Tear, Dendritic Agate, Gold, Malachite, Ruby, Selenite, Tiger Iron
Dangerous - Occupation	Pyrite
Dark Forces	Tourmalinated Quartz
Death	Amethyst, Chalcopyrite
Deception	Apophyllite
Decision Making	Amethyst, Chrysocolla, Labradorite, Lazurite, Onyx
Dedication	Peridot
Deities	Selenite
Delusions	Carnelian Agate
Degenerative Disease	Citrine

Depression	Amethyst, Fluorite, Jet, Kunzite, Peridot, Rhodonite, Smoky Quartz, Rutilated Quartz, Sugilite, Topaz, Tourmalinated Quartz, Zircon
Desire	Jade, Peridot
Destiny	Silver
Determination	Howlite
Detoxification	Azurite with Malachite, Obsidian, & Snowflake Obsidian, Silver, Topaz
Devotion	Tiger Eye
Dexterity	Azurite with Malachite
Detoxify	Clear Quartz
Diabetes	Celestine, Diamond, Emerald, Celestine, Charoite, Chrysocolla
Diarrhoea	Malachite
Difficulties	Carnelian Agate, Zeolite
Digestion	Ametrine Citrine, Chrysocolla, Gold, Jade Pyrite, Topaz
Digestion System	Pyrite, Sodalite, Gold
Diplomacy	Moonstone
Direction	Rutilated Quartz
Disappointment	Carnelian Agate
Discomfort	Turquoise
Discord	Pearl
Disease	Amethyst, Clear Quartz

Divination	Fluorite, Opal, Rutilated Quartz, Sapphire, Silver, Topaz
Dizziness	Sapphire
Doubt	Jade, Jasper -Red
Dreams	Alexandrite, Azurite with Malachite, Clear Quartz, Chrysotile, Jade, Smoky Quartz, Topaz, Zircon
Driving	Pyrite
Drunkenness	Amethyst
Dyslexia	Malachite
Dysplasia	Copal

E

Ears	Amber, Sapphire
Eating Disorders	Kunzite, Unakite
Eczema	Sapphire
Edema	Chalcopyrite
Emergency	Amazonite
Emotional - Abuse	Obsidian, & Snowflake Obsidian
Emotional - Pain	Amethyst, Garnet, Rhodochrosite, Diamond
Emotional - Strain	
Emotional - Turmoil	Peridot

Emotions	Aquamarine, Aventurine, Calcite, Coral, Howlite, Zircon, Silver
Emotions - Frayed	Sapphire
Emotions - Suppressed	Rose Quartz
Emphysema	Rhodonite
Employment	Jasper -Red
Encouraging	Moonstone
Encouragement	Pyrite
Endocrine System	Coral, Sugilite, Tourmalinated Quartz
Endurance	Garnet, Jade
Enemies	Ruby, Tiger Eye
Enlightenment	Copal
Energy	Citrine, Clear Quartz, Chrysocolla, Gold, Hematite, Silver, Rhodochrosite, Rhodonite,
Enthusiasm	Smoky Quartz, Sodalite
Envy	Ruby, Sapphire, Tiger Eye
Empathy	Howlite
Epidemic	Pyrite
Epilepsy	Jasper, Lapis Lazuli, Onyx
Evil	Blue Lace Agate, Petrified Wood

Evil (eye)	Bloodstone, Clear Quartz, Tiger's Eye, Bloodstone
Exams	Citrine, Clear Quartz, Fluorite
Experiences	Charoite, Pyrite
Exercising	Charoite, Garnet
Extraterrestrial	Meteorite
Eyes	Agate, Aquamarine, Charoite, Chrysoprase, Diamond Emerald, Lapis Lazuli, Malachite, Obsidian, & Snowflake Obsidian, Opal
Fainting	Clear Quartz,
Fairy Kingdom	Apophyllite
Faith	Copper
Faithfulness	Agate, Ruby
Falling	Malachite
Fatigue	Amber, Calcite, Citrine, Hematite
Fear	Aquamarine, Aventurine, Blue Quartz, Howlite, Jasper -Red, Silver, Sodalite, Topaz, Tourmalinated Quartz, Unakite
Feelings	Apatite, Sodalite, Unakite
Feet	Apophyllite, Aquamarine

Female - Energy	Aventurine, Meteorite Moonstone, Smoky Quartz, Tourmalinated Quartz, Tiger Eye
Female - Problems	
Fertility	Carnelian, Red Jasper, Tiger's Eye (all together) Dendritic Agate, Chrysoprase, Jade, Silver
Fever	Amethyst, Bloodstone, Diamond, Jasper - Red, Lapis Lazuli Sapphire
Fidelity	Diamond, Tiger Eye
Financial stability	Jet, Moonstone, Loadstone, Opal
Flu	Jet, Topaz
Fluid Retention	Aquamarine
Focus	Clear Quartz, Fluorite
Foetus	Unakite
Food Poisoning	Emerald
Forgetfulness	Fluorite, Moss Agate
Forgiveness	Rose Quartz
Fortune	Aquamarine, Jasper Red, Moonstone, Opal
Fractures	Agate, Howlite, Petrified Wood
Friendship	Bloodstone, Chrysoprase, Citrine
Frustration	Pyrite

Future   Iolite
Fuzzy - Head   Selenite

G

Gallbladder   Selenite, Serpentine
Gallstones   Amethyst
Gastro   Amber, Citrine, Tiger Eye
General Health   Aquamarine
Genitals   Tiger Eye
Gentleness   Moonstone
Glands   Amethyst, Opal, Topaz
Goals   Gold, Howlite, Zircon
Gout   Pyrite
Gracefully   Turquoise
Grazers   Peridot
GRD Syndrome   Ametrine
Greed   Blue Lace Agate
Grief   Amethyst, Onyx, Rhodonite
Grounding   Hematite, Jasper -Red, Obsidian, & Snowflake Obsidian, Petrified Wood, Smoky Quartz, Tiger Iron, Tourmalinated Quartz, Unakite
Growth   Azurite, Kunzite, Lapis Lazuli, Unakite

H

Habits	Amethyst, Blue Lace Agate, Topaz
Haemorrhoids	Amethyst
Hair	Aventurine, Chalcopyrite, Malachite, Petrified Wood
Hands	Aquamarine
Happiness	Agate, Citrine, Emerald, Moonstone, Moss Agate, Onyx, Petrified Wood, Sapphire Smoky Quartz
Harm	Amethyst, Tiger Eye
Harmful Influences	Garnet
Harmony	Hematite, Moonstone, Pearl Rhodonite, Rose Quartz
Hay fever	Zircon
Headaches	Amethyst, Cat's Eye, Celestine, Coral, Hematite, Jet
Healing	Clear Quartz, Copper, Jade, Pyrite, Rose Quartz, Sunstone
Healing - Speed	Rutilated Quartz, Zeolite
Health	Gold, Lapis Lazuli, Sapphire

Heart	Alexandrite, Aquamarine, Aventurine, Charoite, Emerald, Garnet, Hematite, Jade, Kunzite, Malachite, Moldavite Rhodochrosite, Rhodonite, Rose Quartz, Ruby
Heartache	Rhodochrosite
Heartburn	Citrine
Hepatitis	Citrine, Yellow Calcite
High Blood Pressure	Hematite, Kunzite, Lapis Lazuli
Home	Selenite
Hope	Citrine, Loadstone, Jade, Lepidolite, Sugilite
Hormones	Amethyst, Jasper - Red, Moonstone, Sodalite
Hostility	Peridot
Hurt	Unakite
Hypertension	Hematite
Hypnotist	Iolite
Hysteria	Lapis Lazuli

I

Illness	Calcite, Clear Quartz, Copper, Hematite, Unakite, Zeolite
Illness Prevention	Aventurine

Immune System	Lapis Lazuli, Malachite, Rutilated Quartz, Ruby, Sapphire
Insecurity	Peridot
Indigestion	Citrine, Tiger Eye
Indulgence	Bloodstone
Infection	Amethyst, Copper, Smoky Quartz,
Inflammation	Amethyst, Chalcopyrite, Lazurite, Topaz
Inner - Conflict	Sodalite
Inner - Growth	Chrysoprase, Lapis Lazuli
Inner - Peace	Lazurite
Insanity	Amethyst, Citrine, Kunzite
Insight	Azurite
Insomnia	Amethyst, Azurite with Malachite, Lepidolite, Zircon
Inspiration	Agate, Apatite, Aquamarine, Onyx, Sugilite
Intellect	Azurite with Malachite, Rhodochrosite
Interactions	Calcite
Integrity	Tiger Eye
Intestines	Obsidian
Introverts	Blue Quartz
Intuition	Azurite, Citrine, Labradorite, Moonstone, Peridot, Silver, Tiger Eye

Invigorating	Opal
Invincible	Carnelian Agate, Ruby
Irritability	Rhodonite
Irritated throat	Amber, Sodalite
Itching	Amethyst, Malachite

J

Jaundice	Lapis Lazuli, Sodalite
Jealousy	Apophyllite, Chrysoprase, Tourmalinated Quartz
Joint Inflammation	Amethyst, Celestine, Hematite, Lazurite, Celestine, Rhodonite
Joy	Amazonite, Amber, Chrysocolla, Chrysoprase, Moonstone, Ruby
Jumpy	Hematite
Judgement	Sodalite
Justice	Bloodstone

K

Kidneys	Ametrine, Calcite, Kunzite, Rose Quartz, Serpentine, Smoky Quartz
Kindness	Emerald, Kunzite, Selenite, Rose Quartz, Smoky Quartz
Lactation	Coral
Laryngitis	Lapis Lazuli, Sodalite

Legal Battles	Bloodstone
Legs	Aquamarine, Tiger Eye
Lessons	Moldavite
Lethargy	Carnelian, Clear Quartz
Lie	Chrysotile
Life	Aquamarine
Life - Path	Peridot
Listen	Silver
Liver	Alexandrite, Ametrine, Calcite, Tiger Eye, Topaz
Logic	Rose Quartz
Longevity	Amber, Gold
Lost Objects	Chalcopyrite
Love	Aquamarine Calcite, Carnelian Agate Celestine, Chrysotile, Emerald, Jade, Lapis Lazuli, Lepidolite Malachite. Moonstone, Rose Quartz, Ruby, Selenite, Silver, Turquoise Unakite
Love - Attract	Rhodochrosite
Love - Self	Rhodochrosite
Luck	Amber, Apache Tear, Bloodstone, Cat's Eye, Citrine, Pyrite, Ruby, Tiger Eye,
Lumbago	Sapphire
Lung fluid	Amber, Zircon

Lungs	Amber, Aventurine Chrysotile, Rhodonite, Topaz
Lymphatic System	Moonstone

M

Male – Energy	Tourmalinated Quartz
Malignancy	Amethyst, Carnelian Agate
Magic - Intent	Copper
Manic Depression	Kunzite, Lepidolite
Muscular Pain	Aventurine
Masculine Energy	Aventurine
Mathematics	Selenite
Meditation	Amethyst, Aquamarine, Azurite, Calcite, Celestine, Clear Quartz, Copal, Diamond, Fluorite, Kunzite, Meteorite, Moldavite Sapphire, Selenite, Tourmalinated Quartz
Mediums	Iolite,
Memory	Azurite with Malachite, Citrine, Fluorite, Hematite Pyrite
Menopause	Diamond, Ruby
Menstrual - Cycle	Labradorite, Serpentine

Menstrual - Problems	Chrysocolla, Moonstone, Selenite
Menstruation	Aquamarine
Mental Acuity	Jasper - Red
Mental Clarity	Clear Quartz, Gold, Sapphire
Mental Illness	Amethyst, Apatite, Chrysoprase, Fluorite Kunzite, Malachite
Messages - Other Worlds	Moldavite
Metabolism	Sodalite, Topaz
Migraine	Amethyst, Hematite, Rose Quartz, Kunzite
Mind	Zircon, Peridot
Miscarrage	Bloodstone
Mishaps	Chrysoprase
Money	Aquamarine Citrine, Emerald, Loadstone, Pyrite, Red Jasper, Selenite, Serpentine. Tiger Eye
Money - Attract	Gold
Mood	Bloodstone
Moon - Full	Clear Quartz
Motivation	Rhodochrosite
Mundane	Peridot
Muscles	Petrified Wood

Muscular - Development	Tiger Iron
Muscular - Spasms	Diamond, Turquoise
Muscular - Tension	Amethyst, Howlite, Lapis Lazuli, Lepidolite
Music	Apatite
Mathematical Endeavours	Hematite

N

Nails	Howlite
Negative - Behaviour	Malachite
Negative - Energy	Opal, Sapphire
Negative - Thoughts	Obsidian, Sugilite
Negative - Magic	Apache Tear
Negative - Vibration	Tiger Eye

Negativity	Apache Tear, Aquamarine, Azurite with Malachite, Carnelian Agate Cat's Eye, Chrysoprase, Clear Quartz, Garnet, Kunzite, Moonstone, Obsidian, & Snowflake Obsidian, Onyx, Ruby, Smoky Quartz, Tiger Eye Tourmalinated Quartz
Negativity - Repel	Petrified Wood
Nerves	Amazonite, Aquamarine, Hematite, Rhodonite
Nervous - System	Alexandrite, Azurite, Chalcopyrite, Gold, Malachite, Rhodonite, Silver, Topaz
Neurological – Complications	Turquoise
Night - Vision	Tiger Eye
Nightmares	Amethyst
Nursing - Mothers	Howlite, Fluorite
New Beginnings	Moonstone

O

Obesity	Zircon
Objectivity	Fluorite, Silver, Tiger Eye

Obstacles	Carnelian Agate, Obsidian, & Snowflake Obsidian
Opportunity	Bloodstone, Peridot
Optimism	Apache Tear, Citrine
Organs	Alexandrite, Apatite, Chalcopyrite, Moonstone, Rhodochrosite, Sapphire, Sugilite
Osteoporosis	Amazonite, Sunstone
Ovarian Tumours	Copal
Oxygen Circulation	Hematite

P

Pain	Celestine, Howlite, Sunstone, Turquoise
Painters	Alexandrite, Apatite
Pancreas	Alexandrite, Calcite, Charoite, Malachite, Rhodonite, Sodalite, Smoky Quartz, Tiger Eye
Passion	Carnelian Agate, Emerald, Garnet, Ruby, Turquoise,
Past	Iolite
Past Lives	Ametrine, Aquamarine, Aventurine
Past Life - Regression	Petrified Wood, Rutilated Quartz

Path	Silver
Patience	Amethyst, Howlite
Peace	Agate, Amethyst, Blue Quartz, Calcite, Celestine, Chrysocolla, Howlite, Lapis Lazuli, Rhodonite, Rose Quartz, Malachite, Pearl, Petrified Wood, Rhodochrosite, Sapphire, Tiger Iron, Unakite
Perception	Citrine
Personal - Journey	Zeolite
Perspective	Loadstone, Peridot
Persuasive	Turquoise
Phobias	Aquamarine
Physical - Aware	Ruby
Physical - Illness	Cat's Eye, Gold
Physical - Desires	Onyx
Physical – Protection	Lapis Lazuli
Physical - Strength	Diamond
Pigmentation	Chrysocolla
Pineal Gland	Apophyllite, Opal, Sugilite, Zircon
Pituitary Gland	Coral, Opal, Rhodochrosite, Sugilite, Zircon

Plaque	Howlite, Ruby
Pleasure	Citrine, Ruby, Serpentine
Poets	Aquamarine
Poison antidote	Emerald, Zircon
Positive - Energy	Opal
Positive - Outlook	Pyrite
Positive - Thinking	Gold
Positivity	Apache Tear, Loadstone, Selenite
Potential	Apatite, Zircon
Pregnancy	Carnelian, Copal, Howlite, Fluorite, Pearl, Unakite
Present	Iolite
Prosperity	Cat's Eye, Calcite, Celestine, Emerald, Obsidian, & Snowflake Obsidian
Protection	Amethyst, Apache Tear, Clear Quartz, Copper, Pearl, Pyrite, Ruby, Selenite, Sunstone, Tiger's Eye, Turquoise,
Protective	Cat's Eye, Chrysoprase, Jasper -Red, Kunzite, Moonstone, Obsidian, & Snowflake, Obsidian, Pearl, Pyrite, Serpentine, Silver, Tourmalinated Quartz

Psychic	Aquamarine, Azurite, Diamond, Iolite, Lapis Lazuli, Opal, Sapphire, Sunstone
Psychic - Abilities	Azurite, Clear Quartz, Lapis Lazuli, Lepidolite
Psychic - Awareness	Topaz
Psychism	Azurite with Malachite, Emerald, Iolite, Tourmalinated Quartz
Purity	Aventurine, Selenite
Purifying	Meteorite
Quarrels	Diamond

R

Radioactive	Iolite, Malachite, Therapy
Rage	Howlite, Lapis Lazuli
Rationality	Sodalite
Relaxation	Emerald
Realisation - Self	Rutilated Quartz
Realms	Copal
Reason	Celestine
Rebirthing	Unakite
Receptive	Opal, Silver
Refuge	Tiger Iron

Regeneration	Topaz
Rejuvenates	Jasper - Red
Relationships	Aquamarine, Chrysocolla, Citrine, Lapis Lazuli, Smoky Quartz, Unakite
Relaxation	Emerald, Sodalite
Relaxing	Celestine, Lepidolite
Repel Negativity	Onyx
Reproductive Organs	Carnelian Agate
Reproductive - System	Chrysoprase, Moonstone, Unakite
Respiratory - Stress	Rose Quartz
Respiratory System	Chrysotile, Pyrite
Rheumatism	Copper, Petrified Wood, Sunstone
Rheumatoid Arthritis	Fluorite, Sunstone
Rituals	Citrine, Copper, Gold, Silver
Roads	Zeolite

S

Sadness	Amethyst, Rose Quartz, Ruby
Scientists	Topaz

School	Citrine
Seizures	Apache Tear
Self Confidence	Carnelian Agate
Self-Control	Onyx
Self-Esteem	Copper, Diamond, Kunzite, Zircon
Self – Worth	Zircon
Senility	Petrified Wood
Senses	Ametrine
Sensitivity	Emerald, Pearl, Rose Quartz, Tourmalinated Quartz
Sexual - Communication	Sunstone
Sexual - Disease	Zircon
Sexual - Dysfunctions	Serpentine
Sexual - Energy	Carnelian Agate, Onyx, Smoky Quartz, Unakite
Sexual - Imbalance	Cooper, Smoky Quartz
Sexuality	Clear Quartz
Shingles	Chrysoprase
Sickness	Loadstone
Sincerity	Turquoise
Singers	Bloodstone

Skin	Garnet, Petrified Wood, Topaz, Zircon
Sleep	Amethyst, Azurite, Aventurine, Topaz
Smoking	Chrysotile
Sore Eyes	Emerald
Sore Throat	Celestine
Sores	Celestine
Sorrow	Amethyst, Apache Tear, Carnelian Agate
Speaking	Blue Quartz, Rhodochrosite
Spine	Apache Tear
Spirit	Copal
Spirit - Guides	Azurite, Clear Quartz, Iolite
Spirit - World	Moldavite
Spiritual - Awareness	Celestine, Kunzite, Lapis Lazuli, Sodalite, Kunzite, Zeolite
Spiritual - Journey	Celestine, Chrysotile
Spiritual - Love	Sugilite
Spiritual Reading	Cat's Eye
Spleen	Alexandrite, Amber, Calcite, Malachite, Rhodochrosite
Spleen	Alexandrite
Steroid – Production	Tiger Iron

Stomach	Aquamarine, Calcite, Citrine, Selenite, Serpentine, Yellow Topaz
Strength	Aquamarine, Amazonite, Clear Quartz, Copper, Diamond, Hematite, Jasper - Red, Labradorite, Ruby, Pyrite, Tiger Iron
Strength - Inner	Ruby
Stress	Amethyst, Cat's Eye, Chrysoprase, Howlite, Lepidolite, Moonstone, Moss Agate, Obsidian, & Snowflake Obsidian, Peridot, Petrified Wood, Rhodonite, Silver, Sugilite, Topaz
Strokes	Fluorite
Strung	Hematite
Study	Amazonite, Citrine, Clear Quartz, Copper, Garnet
Substance - Abuse	Jade
Surgery	Moldavite
Success	Chrysoprase, Gold
Sugar	Charoite
Surgery	Moldavite
Swimming	Moonstone

T

Talisman	Carnelian Agate
Tarot	Iolite
Taste	Topaz
Technology	Charoite
Teeth	Calcite, Fluorite, Howlite, Selenite, Onyx
Teething	Amber
Telepathic	Meteorite
Temper	Blue Lace Agate, Rose Quartz
Tension	Chrysoprase, Howlite, Lapis Lazuli, Rose Quartz, Selenite, Topaz
Terminal Illness	Chalcopyrite
Testicles	Alexandrite
Third Eye	Opal
Throat	Agate, Carnelian Agate, Celestine, Lazurite, Sodalite, Aquamarine, Rhodonite
Throat Chakra	Blue Quartz
Thyroid	Amber, Citrine, Sodalite
Tiredness	Clear Quartz, Copper, Pyrite
Tissue Regeneration	Alexandrite, Jasper - Red, Malachite, Peridot
Tonsillitis	Amber, Amethyst

Toothache	Aquamarine
Toxins	Charoite, Rose Quartz
Tranquillity	Turquoise
Tranquillity	Amethyst, Aventurine, Blue Quartz, Lapis Lazuli, Malachite, Pearl, Topaz, Turquoise
Transition	Lepidolite, Moonstone
Trauma	Apatite, Rose Quartz
Travel	Calcite, Malachite, Moonstone, Obsidian, & Snowflake Obsidian
True - Path	Malachite
Trustworthy	Turquoise
Trust	Turquoise
Truth	Apophyllite, Celestine, Smoky Quartz
Tumours	Copal
Tumours	Amethyst
Turmoil	Azurite with Malachite, Emerald, Fluorite, Tiger Eye

U

Ulcers	Azurite with Malachite, Amber, Citrine
Understanding	Azurite with Malachite, Celestine, Charoite, Chrysocolla, Rose Quartz, Selenite

Unworthy	Unakite
Upheaval	Petrified Wood
Uplifting	Smoky Quartz, Topaz

V

Varicose Veins	Amber, Aquamarine
Veins	Apache Tear, Obsidian, & Snowflake Obsidian
Venture	Chrysoprase
Verbal Expression	Aquamarine
Vibrations	Celestine
Violence	Amethyst, Bloodstone, Rose Quartz
Vision	Aquamarine, Coral, Meteorite, Opal
Vitality	Ruby, Tiger Iron
Vitamin	Tiger Iron
Vulnerability	Rhodonite

W

Wealth	Moss Agate, Ruby, Selenite, Turquoise
Weight	Unakite
Will Power	Tiger Iron
Wisdom	Jade, Gold, Sugilite

Workplace	Chrysocolla
Worries	Petrified Wood
Writers	Amazonite, Aquamarine, Topaz

Bibliography

Ronald Bonewitz, "*Thorsons Way of Crystal Healing*" Harper Collins, Hammersmith, London, 2001.

Phyllis Galde, "*Crystal Healing: The next step*" Llewellyn Publications, Minnesota, USA, 1996.

Edmund Harold, "*Crystal Healing Helps Restore Harmony of Body and Spirit*" Penguin Books, Australia, 1992.

Raym, "*Alchemy of Crystals*" Global Healing, Byron Bay, Australia, 2000.

Marcia Stark, "*Healing With Astrology*" The Crossing Press, California, USA, 1997.

Doreen Virtue, "*Chakra Clearing*" Hay House, California, USA, 1998.

"*Love is in the Earth, A Kaleidoscope of Crystals 'updated'* " USA - 1995

Ileana Abrev, "*Charm Spells*" Conari Press, US - 2004

Judy Hall, 'The Crystal Bible' 2003

www.ingramcontent.com/pod-product-compliance
Lightning Source LLC
Chambersburg PA
CBHW061727070526
44583CB00024B/3031